the HOMEMAKER'S PICTORIAL ENCYCLOPEDIA

of # modern cake decorating

BORDERS · FLOWERS · FIGURE PIPING · TUBE WRITING · GUM
PASTE · SUGAR MOLD · COOKIES · PASTRIES · SANDWICHES ·
PETITS FOURS · CREAM PUFFS · HORS D'OEUVRES · SALADS ·
DESSERTS · SPUN SUGAR · PULLED SUGAR · CANDY

by

Authors

McKINLEY WILTON & NORMAN WILTON

Published By

McKINLEY WILTON AND NORMAN WILTON

Wilton Enterprises, 11008 South Halsted St., Chicago, Illinois

Also Publishers of "Wilton Wonderland of Cake Decorating" and "Party Cakes U.S.A."

PRINTED IN THE UNITED STATES OF AMERICA

Dedicated to the
American Homemaker
Who Constantly Searches
for Better Ways
to Serve Her
Family and Friends.

1st printing, October, 1954—10,000
2nd printing June, 1955—10,000
3rd printing February, 1956—10,000
4th printing May, 1956—10,000
5th printing November, 1956—10,000
6th printing May, 1957—10,000
7th printing November, 1957—10,000
8th printing February, 1958—10,000
9th printing June, 1958—10,000
10th printing January, 1959—10,000
11th printing March, 1959 — 10,000
12th printing September, 1959—10,000
13th printing March, 1960—10,000
14th printing May, 1960—13,000
15th printing September, 1960—10,000
16th Printing September, 1961 — 10,000
17th Printing February, 1962 — 10,000

The authors wish to thank
The Schram Advertising Company, Chicago, Illinois,
for their valuable assistance in preparing this book.

MR. McKINLEY WILTON . . . world's most renowned Cake Decorator and Fine Candy Maker. Founder and President of the famous Wilton School of Cake Decorating and Fine Candy Making. Originator of the Modern Techniques of Master Cake Decorating and Pulled Sugar Work.

MR. NORMAN WILTON . . . Famed Cake Decorator and Fine Candy Maker. The finest Pulled Sugar Work Artist in the country. Vice-President and Instructor of the Wilton School. Nationally known lecturer and demonstrator of Modern Cake Decorating Techniques.

The staff of the Wilton School—reading from left to right: McKinley Wilton, Martha Wilton Ellison, Norman Wilton, Mary Wilton, Wesley Wilton. Each member of the renowned Wilton Family shown here is an outstanding decorator and teacher. For the first time their combined knowledge is made available to the general public in this easy-to-understand, complete Encyclopedia of Modern Cake Decorating and Fine Candy Making.

THE WILTON SCHOOL

The teaching record of the Wilton School is the greatest endorsement of the Wilton methods and the Wilton standing in the Cake Decorating and Fine Candy Making fields.

Not only have over 4,000 professional bakers attended the School, but the student body has also comprised thousands of hotel chefs, home economists, home-arts teachers, dieticians, hobbyists and home makers.

Students have come from every state in the Union and from many foreign countries as well.

Periodically the Wilton School "takes to the road" and travels world-wide to hold classes. Wilton classes have been held in Hawaii, Japan, India, and in most of the countries in Europe and in Great Britain. In these countries it is the old-world masters who come to the Wiltons for the newest techniques and developments of Modern Cake Decorating.

Introduction

We believe this is the most complete and practical book ever written on the subject of Modern Cake Decorating and Fine Candy Making for the home maker who wishes to learn these arts in her own kitchen.

This book follows the Wilton Techniques as taught at the famous Wilton School of Cake Decorating. It has been written so that the homemaker who has had little or no experience can easily learn to decorate cakes, salads, fruit plates, hors d'oeuvres, etc., beautifully and professionally.

The Wilton Method of Teaching is a "do-it-yourself" method. Emphasis has been placed on large, detailed illustrations with just the necessary amount of easy-to-read, easy-to-understand and easy-to-follow instructions. Thumb through the book. You will be amazed at the large number of beautiful illustrations showing every step of the decorating process.

Believing in "first things first" we begin with the simple but necessary equipment you will need, the types of icings, the "why's" and "when's" for using them . . . and then to the first simple steps of Cake Decorating.

These are followed by simple border work designs. Then beautiful life-like flowers are shown and explained. We proceed to the easiest cake top designs and then to larger special cake arrangements. New and simple methods of Figure Piping and Color Technique used exclusively by the Wiltons are revealed. There are hundreds of illustrated ideas for cake tops and floral arrangements.

All phases of the decorating process are fully illustrated and clearly explained.

Everything taught at the Wilton School has been included in this book. There is a chapter devoted to Spun and Pulled Sugar Work, and a chapter on Fine Candy Making.

With a little practice, following the Wilton Techniques written for you in this book, you will become a remarkably proficient and accomplished decorator and you will soon be turning out decorated pieces of professional quality.

Your decorated pieces will be the envy of your friends and the topic of conversation among your guests. And you will be amazed at the personal satisfaction, the wonderful sense of creating something rare and beautiful, every time you decorate a cake.

Table of Contents

CHAPTER I

Fundamentals

ICING THE CAKE

As a first step in our study of cake decorating, we will examine the methods and materials of icing a cake. The icing or frosting serves as the setting for the decorations and is actually the initial step in the decorating process.

Frosting helps keep the cake moist. It is important to have your cake cold and free from crumbs before it is frosted. When frosting layer cakes, lay four strips of waxed paper on a plate or doilie as illustrated. Invert one layer, spread filling evenly over this, then place the second layer on top and frost. If you are using a thin icing, you may start by pouring the icing on the top and then work to the sides. In using a heavier icing such as a marshmallow or buttercream, we prefer to start on the sides first and then go to the top of the cake as illustrated. The spatula may be dipped in hot water if a very smooth effect is desired. Here are a few effects that may be obtained by following the simple instructions.

SPIRAL EFFECT

The spatula is held at the center of the cake. Turn the cake slowly with the left hand and move the spatula gradually to the outer edge of the cake.

FLUFFY STUCCO EFFECT

A boiled or marshmallow icing should be used. After the cake is iced the spatula is placed on the cake and then pulled away to make a series of peaks.

ZIG-ZAG PATTERN

Cut saw-like teeth along the edge of a cardboard approximately the same width as the cake. Take the cardboard in both hands, as illustrated, and start at the edge of the cake moving the cardboard along the cake top using a series of side to side motions.

The stencil cake is first iced with a hard drying icing. The desired pattern is cut out of cardboard and placed on the cake top. The pattern is then iced over in a contrasting color using a spatula knife.

The Spider Web effect was obtained as follows. First ice the cake in any desired color. Then with three ounces of melted bitter chocolate in a small cone with a No. 3 tube, start a series of circles working from the outer edge of the cake. Draw a knife lightly over the cake as illustrated giving the desired effect.

Chocolate Drip Effect cake is iced in a hard drying icing and chocolate is poured over the cake as illustrated.

DECORATING ICINGS

Realizing the housewife has many favorite frostings for her cakes we will concentrate on decorating icings.

No matter how you practice decorating and how much equipment you have, your icing must be at the right consistency or all your decorating efforts will be in vain.

When working with a decorating icing, it is often necessary to vary the consistency of your particular icing. If you are practicing a simple border, your icing should be of a medium consistency. For many of the different types of flowers, a stiffer icing is required in order to make the petal stand up and have a more lifelike effect. All of our decorating formulas are worked out to give you a medium stiff consistency and they may be used for either flowers or borders. Where you are told to thin down the icing slightly, do so by adding a few drops of water. Now the question arises, where would a thinned down icing be used? In string work and tube writing the icing must be of a thinner consistency in order to draw out properly. If a heavy, stiff

icing is used, as pressure is applied to the cone the icing will tend to break as it is moved along the surface of the cake. By using a thinner icing it will tend to string out and much better results will be obtained. It is very important that you follow our icing recipes in detail, for without the proper icing or the proper consistency all of your practice and our instructions will be in vain.

There are three main types of decorating icing. The *buttercream*, the *boiled* and *royal* icing.

All of the following icings were tested on a standard home electric mixer. Heavy duty mixers will require 3 to 4 minutes less beating time per each step. It is important to remember all utensils must be completely free of grease.

Keep in mind that these icings are for decorating and must be stiff. If you are using the proper ingredients there are only two things that would make your icing fail: 1. Not beating long enough

    2. A tiny amount of grease in your batch.

ROYAL ICING WITH MERINGUE POWDER

Royal Icing is the choice of professional bakers for all phases of cake decorating. It can be easily made from the preparation, Wilton Deluxe Meringue. Royal Icing is used for decorating only, never for the frosting or icing of cakes. It is preferred chiefly because of its stiff, firm consistency—excellent for forming clear, sharp outlines and crisper flowers. Flowers and decorations of Royal Icing can be made, dried and kept without refrigeration for months. There is no waste, ever . . . add coloring to only what you need and store the balance in a sealed container and refrigerate. When needed, just whip with a beater to restore original consistency. Royal Icing is greaseless and dissolves quickly, thereby eliminating much of the mess of cleaning-up.

    ¼ cup water
    3 teaspoons Meringue
    1¾ cups 10X Confectioners Sugar (Powdered)*

Whip for 5 minutes at high speed. Keep covered with damp cloth. Icing should stand to 3-4 inch peak on spatula knife, if icing begins to fall slightly after lengthy use, simply rewhip.

*3¾ cups of Confectioners Sugar to one pound.

For a lighter icing, add a tablespoon of water and continue beating. The addition of water and continued beating makes this icing even lighter than boiled icing. When your flowers harden from this lightly beaten icing, they must be handled very carefully because the air cells in the icing tend to crumble.

Use this icing when you are making up flowers or various decorations in advance. The icing will dry and you may peel it off your waxed paper and place your decorations on cakes, petits fours, etc. without damaging your decorations.

ROYAL ICING MADE WITH EGG WHITE

3 egg whites (room temperature)
1 lb. confectioners sugar
½ teaspoon cream of tartar

The above ingredients are placed in mixing bowl and beaten for 7 to 10 minutes.

This icing is a hard drying icing. Keep covered with damp cloth at all times.

This is used in the same way as the Royal icing with meringue powder, but it will not give as much volume and will not beat up as well for use at a later date.

DECORATING BUTTER CREAM

    1 cup vegetable shortening
    1½ cups confectioners sugar
    ¼ cup evaporated milk

Cream at high speed for 5 minutes.

For tastier icing, use half butter and half shortening. To thin down the icing for inscriptions and borders, add a few drops of liquid. Store in airtight container in the refrigerator. Whip up before using the second time.

Flowers made up in advance using this recipe should be placed in the refrigerator to harden slightly and become easy to handle.

FRENCH BUTTERCREAM

This is a very delicious and unusual buttercream to be used for cake or French pastries. This buttercream has as smooth a texture as whipped cream, and is really delicious.

Make a batch of either of our boiled icing recipes. Spread in sheet pan and let cool completely. Fold in (do not beat) ⅛ lb. of butter at room temperature.

If a thinner consistency is desired, add a few drops of cream.

BOILED ICING WITH MERINGUE POWDER

(A) 2 level tablespoons of meringue powder
    ¼ cup of water
(B) 1 cup of granulated sugar
    ¼ cup of water
    ⅛ teaspoon Cream of Tarter
(C) 1 cup of confectioner's sugar (powdered)

Mix (A) together by pouring water into bowl and adding meringue powder. Beat at high speed for 7 minutes. Place (B) ingredients in saucepan and boil to 240 degrees.

After beating mixture (A) for 7 minutes, turn to low speed and add (C). Beat together 2 minutes at high speed. When (B) reaches 240 degrees add slowly to mixture (A) and (C), and beat together at high speed for 5 minutes.

Add ½ teaspoon of desired flavoring.

Boiled Icing may be kept for one week or more if placed in an air tight container or sealed with damp cloth over a bowl. To reuse, simply beat, do not add any ingredients. This icing is ideal for flower and border work, as it will never run or weep regardless of weather. To prevent crusting—keep icing covered with damp cloth at all times.

BOILED ICING USING EGG WHITES

(A) 2 cups granulated sugar.
     ½ cup of water.
     ¼ teaspoon of cream of tartar.

(B) 4 egg whites (at room temperature).

(C) 1½ cups of sifted confectioners sugar

Cook "A" to 240 degrees. do not let mixture crystallize on the sides of the pan. You can prevent this from happening by washing the sides of the pan down with warm water and a brush. Repeat the washing-down process about halfway through being careful *not* to stir the batch.

While the sugar is boiling place "B" in a mixing bowl and whip at high speeds for 7 minutes. Pour "A" in slowly and whip for 3 minutes more. Turn down to second speed and add "C" gradually. Turn back to high speed and whip the entire contents for 5 minutes more.

You will not be able to rebeat this icing on the following day and have it regain its stiff consistency as you do when using our meringue powder.

Keep covered with damp cloth while using.

Ornamenting tubes are the tools basic to decorating cakes and general ornamenting. Although there are nearly 100 tubes in use today, all practical needs are met through the use of the 10 tubes described in this book. The authors have developed and are marketing a cake decorating kit designed especially for the readers of this book. This kit includes these 10 basic tubes, all of which are shown below.

Every border and flower shown in this book, no matter how intricate or complicated it looks, was made with these simple tubes. Keeping this in mind, you can see that decorating skill comes from careful pressure control—the squeezing and relaxing of pressure on the cone. With smooth, co-ordinated movements of the nail and the cone, almost any flower can be made. With the will to learn and the proper instruction, you can become an expert in the field of fine cake decorating. Any type of material may be used for decorations as long as it flows through the cone or the tube and will hold its shape. In preparing your various materials for decorating, keep in mind the consistency of your icings. If the substance goes through the tube and loses its form, then it is too thin. If too much pressure is required to push it through the tube, then your substance must be thinned down slightly. With this in mind, we shall proceed with the uses of the tube.

No. 3 Tube

This tube is used for writing on a cake top, string work, and many types of figure piping, such as the Swan, Bird and Stork. We also use this tube for making our stems on our cake tops or when any type of small fine work is required.

No. 4 Tube

This tube is used for figure piping of larger objects such as the Clown, Witch, Baby Booties and many types of scrolls where a slightly larger opening is required.

Many types of border work may also be made using this tube, as will be fully illustrated in detail under *Border Work*.

No. 16 Star Tube

This tube is used in many different variations of border work and for heavier types of scroll work that go on the side of a cake and also in some cases for a heavy string work.

One of the first simple flowers that we shall make will be made with this tube, as illustrated above.

No. 190 Tube

The No. 190 tube is used for making drop flowers. A five petal flower is made simply by squeezing and turning. By changing color and stamen, many different varieties of flowers can be formed. Using pink, an Apple Blossom; white for an Orange Blossom; purple for the Violet.

No. 30 Star Tube

This tube is used for a Shell Border, Rope Border, Small Rosettes, and a number of very simply constructed flowers. With the proper pressure control, using a simple squeeze and a stop, it is possible to make many dainty flowers, as will be illustrated in detail under *Flower Making*.

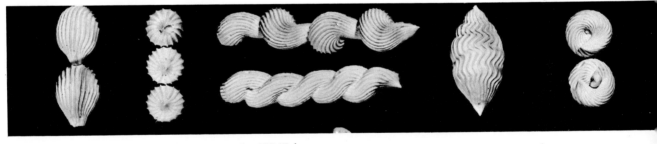

No. 199 Tube

This tube is similar to your No. 30 star tube except that the opening is slightly larger and has many tiny cuts at the tip of the opening. We will use this tube on a number of larger type borders as illustrated and also a number of small flowers can be made very simply using this tube.

No. 67 Leaf Tube

As the name implies, this tube is used in making a leaf. The size of the leaf depends on the amount of pressure that is applied in squeezing the cone. By moving the tube along as you squeeze, a longer leaf may be formed as shown. This tube also may be used for variations in border designs.

No. 103 Tube

This tube is used for many different types of smaller flowers, such as the tiny rose bud, apple blossom, daisy or dahlia. Whenever working on small objects such as petits fours or cupcakes, a small tube such as this will be required in making a number of flowers. This tube may also be used for various types of border work, which will be illustrated in detail in later chapters.

No. 104 Tube

This is the most important and versatile of decorating tubes. As many as 20 different flowers are formed with this simple tube. The Sweetpea, Half Rose, Yellow Jonquil, Carnation, Pansy are just a few of the many flowers that are made using this tube. Many border variations are also made with this tube.

No. 124 Tube

This tube is very similar to the smaller No. 104 tube and is used to make all of our larger flowers. A few of the flowers are illustrated above, such as the Briar Rose, the large American Beauty Rose and even the Orchid. A number of large borders will also be made using this tube.

The Flower Nail

This is a flower nail and is used in conjunction with various tubes to form many types of flowers and decorations. This nail is held with the thumb and forefinger. The nail is turned in a counter-clockwise direction. When making a flower from a hard drying icing, an inch and a half square of waxed paper is placed on the nail. This is done by placing a dot of icing on the nail and sticking the waxed paper to it. By holding your cone of icing in your right hand, and applying pressure, the petals are formed on your nail. As the pressure is applied, the nail is turned, thus forming a petal. When the flower is completed, slide the waxed paper off the nail onto a pan and after drying, the flower is peeled from the waxed paper. Using this method as many flowers as desired may be made using the one nail.

In your first few efforts working with a nail, you will find it difficult to turn the nail in a smooth co-ordinated movement. But with a little practice you will become very proficient.

If you are making a flower in buttercream or a softer type icing, the flower is made directly on the nail and is lifted off with a pair of scissors. This is possible only when making the larger flowers. If a very tiny flower was made in this manner, directly on the nail, it would be impossible to lift the flower off the nail without damaging the flower.

CONSTRUCTING A PAPER CONE

The one thing that discourages a beginner from using paper cones is not knowing how to construct one properly. With five minutes practice, you can become very proficient in making a cone.

The idea is to roll the paper into a cone-like shape. The tip of the cone is cut off, and the tube is dropped inside the cone. This cone is then filled with a decorating icing and closed up by folding or rolling over. Although any type of paper can be used, the best is a vegetable parchment. If this is not obtainable, waxed paper may be used. The heavier the waxed paper, the easier it is to construct the cone. Brown wrapping paper is satisfactory if not used for any great length of time. It absorbs moisture and will break when wet. Vegetable parchment comes in various sizes and cuts.

A recent development in the art of cake decorating is the introduction of flexible and transparent plastic cones. These cones offer several important advantages —they are strong and easily handled, the plastic may be washed and the cones re-used many times. The kit prepared by the authors for the readers of this book includes these new plastic cones.

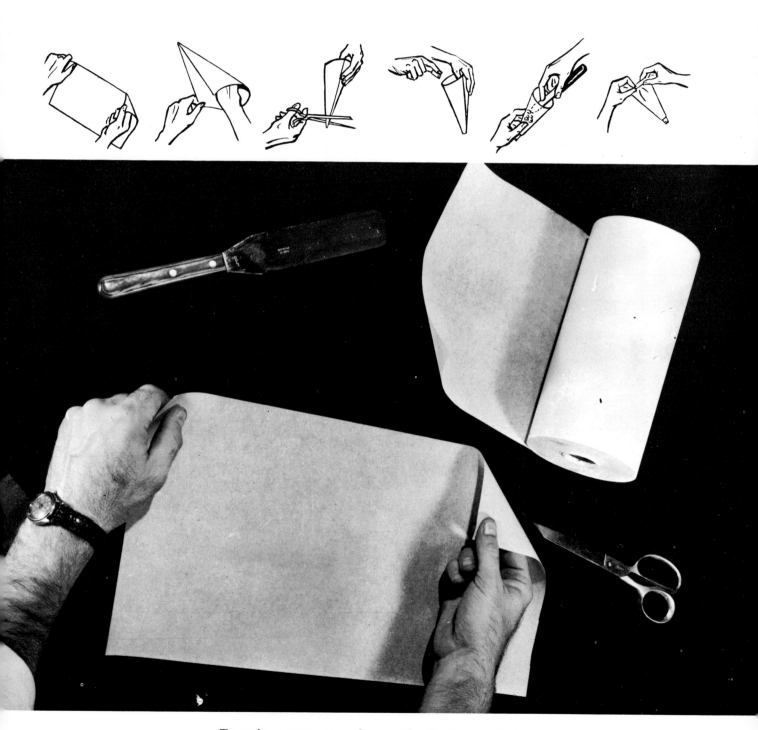

To make a paper cone, from a 9″ roll of paper, first roll out a sheet approximately 17″ long. Lay the sheet of paper flat on a table. Grasp the outer edges between your thumb and forefinger.

Turn the right hand corner and roll the right hand until
a partial cone is formed.

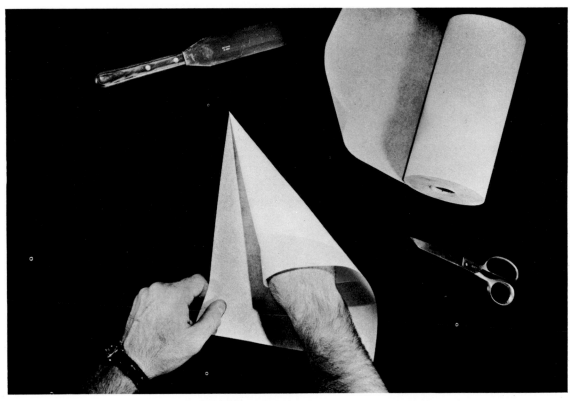

Circle the right hand with the left hand. Move your
hands back and forth to adjust the point of the cone
until it is needle sharp.

After the cone is formed, hold the completed cone firmly, *at the top* with thumb and fingers as shown in the illustration. Cut off the tip about ½ to ¾ inches from the end, depending on the size of the tube you are using. Drop tube into cone.

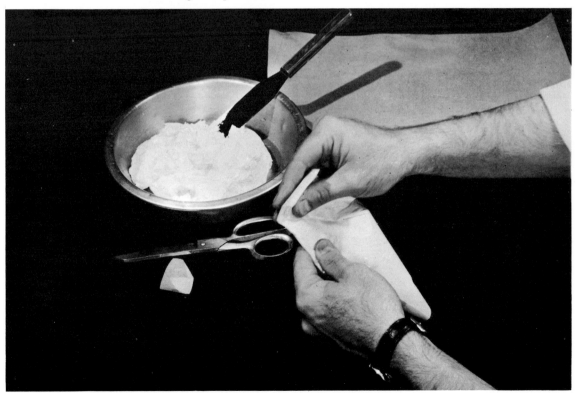

Do not fill the cone over ¾ full. After the cone is full, the top of the cone is folded in. This keeps the icing from backing out of the cone as pressure is applied.

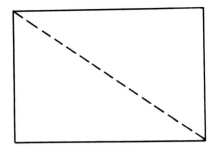

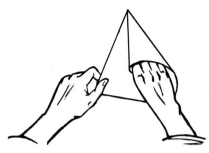

For a small cone, an oblong piece of parchment paper may be cut in half and the same procedure followed using the long side of the triangle to construct the cone. As the cone becomes empty, it is necessary to continue folding the top down as the icing is forced out.

TUBE WRITING
The cone is held with the thumb and two fingers. Pressure is applied thru fingers and thumb. The cone is held at a 45 degree angle to the writing surface.

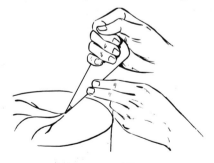

STEMS
When making stems or stamens on flowers the small cone is held in the above position. The entire hand is used to apply pressure.

STRING WORK
When working on the side of a cake or doing fine string work a more controlled pressure is obtained by holding the cone with thumb and two fingers.

PROPER METHOD OF HOLDING A CONE. DETAILS OF PRESSURE CONTROL

After you have constructed your cone, place your tube in it and fill the cone with icing. The next, and most important step, is to apply pressure to the cone so that the icing will flow out the tip. You might imagine that you can simply take a tube full of icing and give it a squeeze and the icing will simply flow out the proper end. You will find on your first few attempts that this is not the case. Before applying pressure to the cone, be sure cone is folded properly to eliminate back-flow of icing.

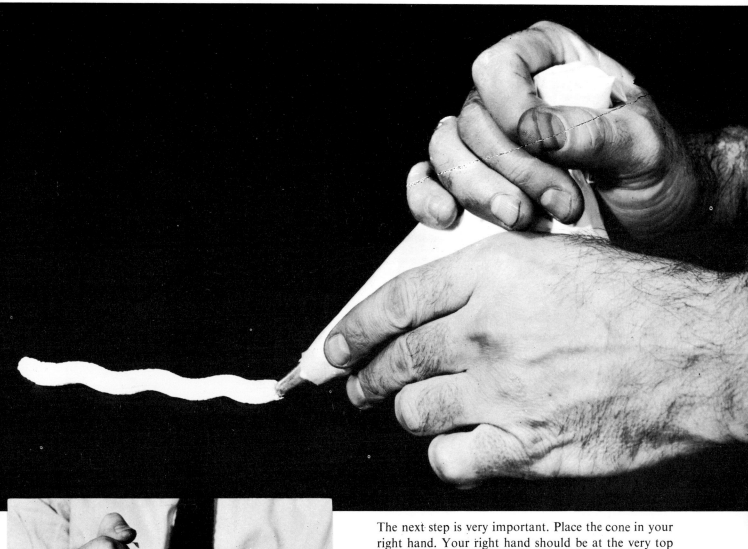

The next step is very important. Place the cone in your right hand. Your right hand should be at the very top of the cone as illustrated. The first two fingers of the left hand are used to guide or steady the cone. In teaching many students to decorate, we find that there is a tendency to use the left hand for holding the cone and also quite often the student will tend to squeeze with the left hand. If this procedure is followed, it is impossible to move the cone in a free easy glide and would also tend to push the icing out the wrong end of the cone.

For most of the border work, the cone is held at an angle of 45 degrees to the working surface as illustrated.

Illustrated is the proper method of holding the cone while working on a flower nail. The tube is held at a 45 degree angle from the surface. This position is explained in detail under *Flowers*.

Illustrates the tube being held perpendicular. For a position such as this the cone is still held in the same manner and the left hand is used again as a guide.

Some very simple borders and flowers will be made and explained in detail with the tube held in this manner.

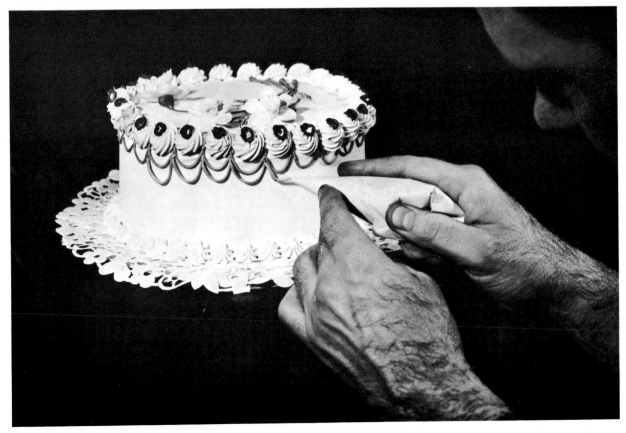

Illustrates the proper method of holding the cone when working on the side of a cake or when writing on a cake top. Notice that a very small cone is being used and that the pressure is applied at the top of the cone with the thumb. The left finger is used as a guide.

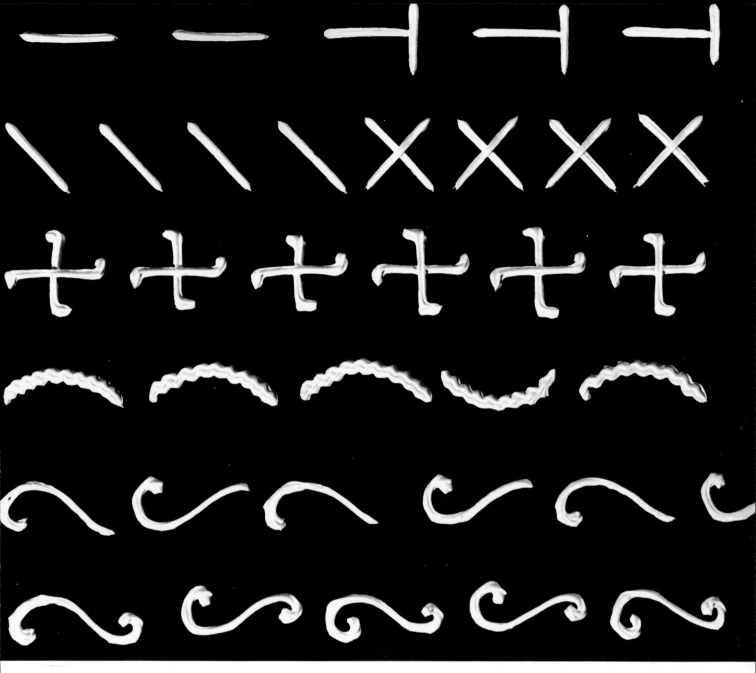

EXERCISE No. 1

Step No. 1. Using the same No. 16 star tube, hold the tube at a 45 degree angle and touch the pan. Apply pressure with the right hand and draw a straight line approximately 2 inches long. As the tube is moved along, an easy, continuous pressure must be applied. If the icing breaks, it is because you have relaxed pressure. If your icing builds up or pushes from side to side, it is because you are applying too much pressure. Continue this straight line and then try crossing the line as illustrated.

Step No. 2 is a series of lines going off at an angle. The line starts at the top and moves down at a 45 degree angle. To cross this line and make an X the tube must be lifted up slightly as you move over your first line.

Step No. 3 is a series of crosses with a slight curlicue on the end. These various movements will help you change directions while continuing pressure on the cone.

Step No. 4. This series of exercise is accomplished by making a slight curve while moving the tube in a side to

side motion. After practicing three movements in the same direction try reversing the direction as illustrated, in step No. 3 of this exercise.

Step No. 5, the tube must be touching the pan slightly at all times. A steady easy movement must be maintained in order to make a uniform design. The first curve is to the right, stop squeezing. The second curve is to the left and so on. You will encounter some difficulty to begin with in knowing when to start to apply pressure and knowing when to stop applying pressure as you come to the end of your movement you will tend to continue squeezing which will draw your lines out too long.

Step No. 6, a curve is started in the same way as above except a slight reverse curve is worked in at the end of the exercise. The first one is started off from the left side and the next one from the right side. This exercise will help you reverse your design as you use a continuous even pressure.

EXERCISE NO. 2

Rest the No. 16 tube on your pan at a 45 degree angle. Apply pressure and move the tube along in a slight curving motion. If the icing tends to build up or become stretched out, it is because you are varying the pressure of your cone or the speed you are moving along the pan.

Step No. 2. For this movement, the same amount of pressure is applied to the cone while maintaining the side to side motion.

Step No. 3. This exercise will give you practice in breaking off or discontinuing your lines. If you find that when you stop, your icing tends to continue flowing from the tip of the tube, it is because you are not completely discontinuing your pressure. Now try it once more.

Step No. 4. For this particular design a slight loop movement is maintained while continuing an even pressure on your cone.

Step No. 5. A line is first drawn out as in exercise No. 1. After the line is drawn the small curled designs are then worked in as illustrated. A small dot is placed upon each curl which forms a design which may be used on the side of a cake.

Step No. 6. A long curved line is first drawn on your pan. Again the tube is held at a 45 degree angle. After this line is formed, tiny dots using the same tube are worked off each curve as illustrated.

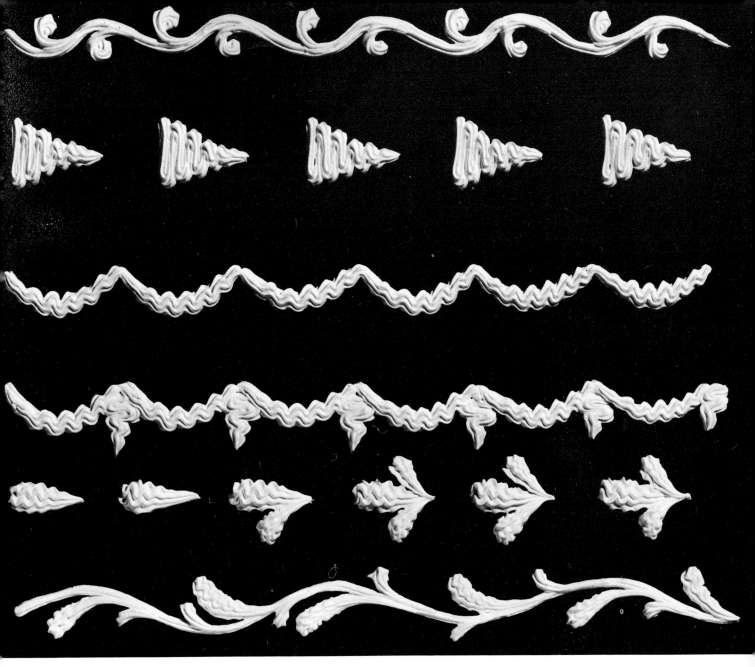

EXERCISE No. 3

Step No. 1. Using the same No. 16 star tube a long curving line is first drawn on your pan. This is formed by moving your tube slightly from side to side as you draw your tube along your pan. The small curlicues worked into each of the curves are formed by first making a dot on the pan, turning slightly and working into the line as you relax pressure. When you have finished this exercise, these small curlicues should work into the first line so smoothly that it is impossible to tell it was made after the first line was drawn.

Step No. 2. This series of exercises are completed by applying the same amount of pressure to your cone as you move your tube along diminishing your side to side motion forming a triangle. This will give you practice in changing the direction of your movement while continuing pressure and yet forming a definite design.

Step No. 3. This series of exercise is accomplished by moving the tube in a slight side to side motion, while following a curved pattern.

Step No. 4. The same procedure is followed as in the above exercise. After this is completed where each of the curves are attached, the tube is placed in the center, pressure is applied and the tube is moved from side to side and is drawn down.

Step No. 5. Touch the pan holding the tube at a 45 degree angle. Apply pressure and move the tube slowly in a side to side motion. As the icing builds up, relax pressure slightly and then diminish pressure to bring icing off to a point. Continue this a few times and then work in smaller curves into each side of the design, as illustrated. This will give you practice in building up your icing designs.

Step No. 6. A slight curved line is first drawn along your pan. The built up lines worked into the pattern are placed on in the same manner as the above exercise.

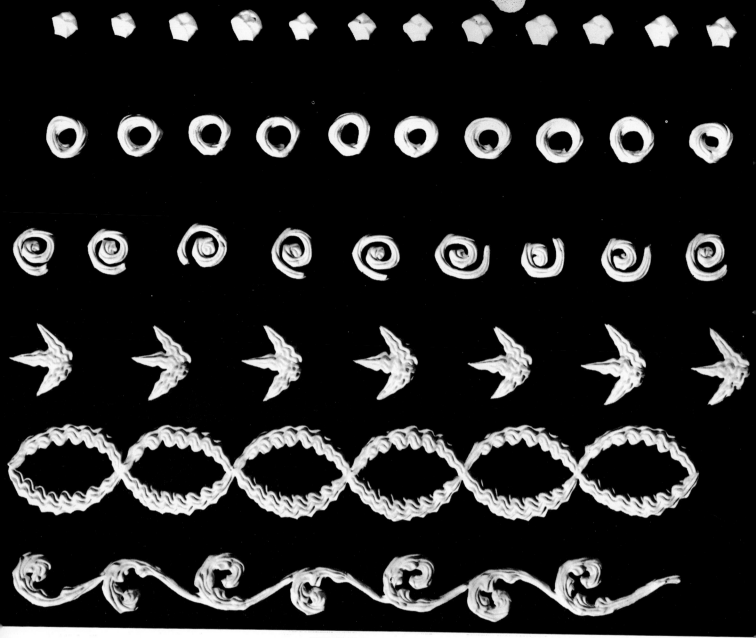

EXERCISE No. 4

Step No. 1. Hold your No. 16 star tube perpendicular to your pan. Apply pressure, discontinue pressure and pull away. If the dot tends to stretch out from your pan it is because you do not relax pressure completely before moving your tube away from your pan.

Step. No. 2. Touch your pan, apply pressure and make a circular motion. As you complete your circle discontinue pressure and continue moving in a circle. This will break your icing off in an even uniform circle, as illustrated.

Step No. 3. Holding the cone perpendicular to the pan, apply pressure, start an easy circular movement as illustrated. The tube must be touching the pan slightly at all times.

Step No. 4. The center design is started first. Holding the tube at a 45 degree angle, apply pressure and move your tube along diminishing pressure as you go. The same procedure is followed for the two lines moving off to an angle. First heavy pressure and then light pressure as you continue moving along.

Step No. 5. This series of exercises is accomplished by following a curved motion starting with a very gentle pressure then increasing this pressure and moving your tube back and forth slightly. Where the curved line diminishes in size the pressure is decreased.

Step No. 6. The scroll design is accomplished by first drawing the design out with a No. 16 star tube. The design is then gone over using the same tube in a series of circular motions while pressure is applied.

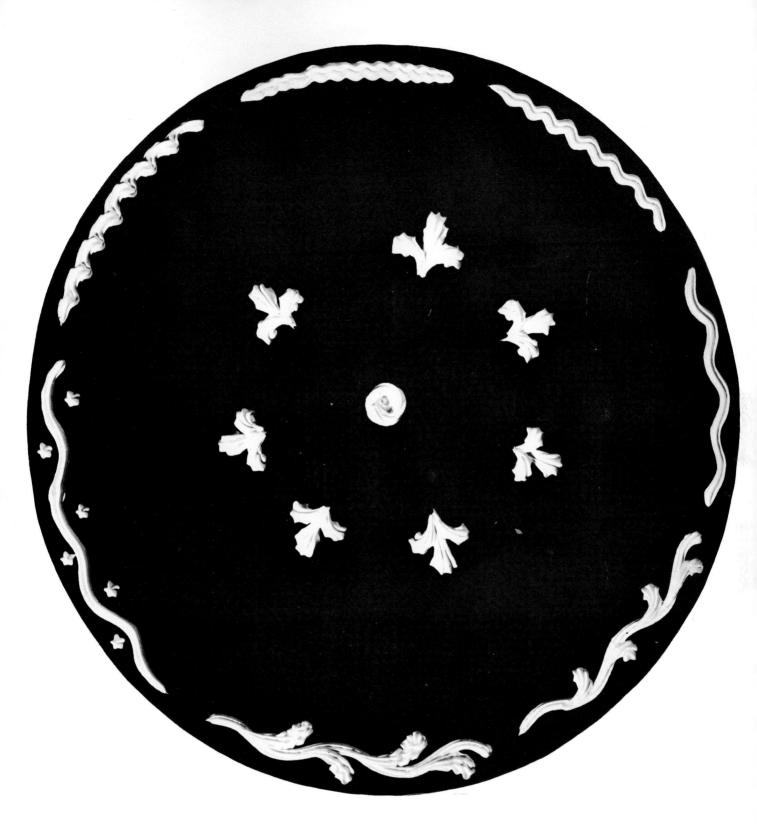

After working with all of your pressure controls on a pan, we suggest you try a few simple exercises on a pie tin. This will give you practice decorating on a simulated cake top.

Fill a No. 16 Star Tube with white icing. Work approximately ½″ from the edge of the pan.

These first exercises are easy side-to-side movements. The problem is to keep the forms an even distance from the edge of the tin and evenly spaced.

Place a rosette in the center. Use the rosette as a focus point and work in the seven small designs around it.

This simulated cake top was decorated entirely with a No. 16 Star Tube. These designs are made in the same manner used when working on your pressure controls.

The purpose of this exercise is to help you obtain uniformity and neatness. Be careful with your spacing and you will have a neatly finished cake top.

In practicing these variations of pressure control you will have more success when making the longer forms. This is because you get into the rhythm of doing one particular movement. Keep this in mind when you start working with the more advanced borders. Do one thing at a time around the entire cake when working on any particular border. Then, when the first step is completed start the second phase of your border and so on.

Changing tubes and movements on each section of any border will tend to slow you down, and even more important—it will be impossible to keep your decorating uniform.

In this exercise, you change pace with each new form, so do not become discouraged if your cake pan looks a little uneven.

COLOR TECHNIQUES

There are three forms of food coloring on the market—paste, liquid and powdered.

Paste colors are preferred for several reasons, and paste colors are used and recommended by all professional decorators for the same reasons.

Paste colors will not change the consistency of your icings as liquid colors will do. They are much stronger, giving you deeper, darker colors. Paste colors are more concentrated—with a little going a long way. Paste colors can and are being used to make liquid colors. Paste colors come in jars and tubes. The Wilton paste colors are packaged in tubes for more convenient handling, less waste and elimination of the danger of colors mixing.

BLENDING AND MIXING PASTE COLORS

To add paste colors to your icing, the following steps should be followed.

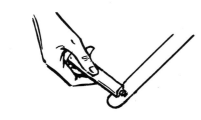

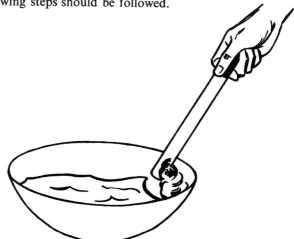

1. Cut a small portion of icing from the main body of icing in your bowl, and keep it separated along the side of the bowl. Place a small dab of paste color on your spatula-knife.

2. Mix the paste into the small portion of icing on the side of your bowl. Be careful not to mix it in with the main portion of icing in this step.

3. Mix the small portion thoroughly and add paste color as necessary to get the shade of coloring desired. It is better to get a slightly deeper shade at this point for when you mix it into the entire contents of the bowl, it will of course become a lighter color.

4. Stir the small portion of icing into the contents of the rest of the bowl, mixing it thoroughly so the color is evenly blended through the entire icing.

IMPORTANT—If another color must be added to obtain a particular shade, repeat the steps outlined in 1 to 3, before you stir the first portion into the rest of the icing in your bowl.

HOW TO MIX AND BLEND COLORED ICINGS

While the importance of the proper use of color in cake decorating cannot be overemphasized, it should also be mentioned here that the simple principles can be easily learned and once learned can be applied with unvarying success to even the most ambitious cake decorating project.

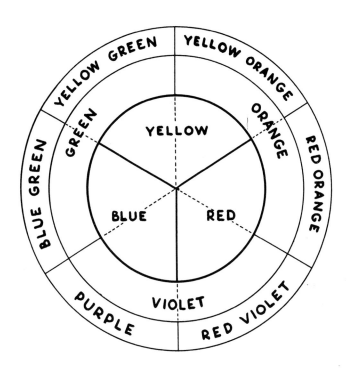

COLOR

Before actually going into the subject of colored icings, a short discussion of color itself may be in order. The full study of color can, of course, occupy a lifetime, but in its application to cake decorating it may be greatly simplified. To begin with, the same rules that apply to the mixing of the artist's colors apply as well to food coloring. When the artist wants green he mixes the proper proportions of blue and yellow, and when the picture calls for violet he merely mixes red and blue. A glance at the "color wheel" illustrated at right will show how all the possible color combinations are made from the three primary colors—blue, yellow and red.

COLORED ICING

Although several coloring agents are available, *paste colors* have been found to be the most generally satisfactory. The range of colors available to the decorator, in addition to the primaries—red, blue and yellow—include violet, green, brown and pink. The color wheel, of course, shows us that we can get along very well with only the 3 primaries.

In using paste colors, it is well to remember that a little goes a long way. A relatively small amount of the intense paste color will tint a large amount of white icing. The *colored icing* and *not* the paste colors are used in mixing other colors, since paste colors by themselves are too intense for accurate color blending. We do, however, use paste colors full strength when we add them to water to prepare a colored spray. The illustrations on the preceding page demonstrate step by step the approved method of color mixing and blending.

Throughout this book we describe the colors used in various decorations. The color wheel tells us how to obtain any color from various combinations of the three primary colors. It remains now to modify the colors obtained (dark or light—warm or cold) to suit our requirements. For example: we mix a small amount of blue icing and a small amount of yellow icing and blend the two together to obtain a green icing. Chances are that the resulting color will be too deep (too green) for, let us say, spring foliage. We simply add more yellow to the mixture to get a "spring" green and then blend in enough white icing to obtain the light tint required.

After we have learned to produce any color we require, we can then consider some refinements in the use of color. For example: a cake decorated with bright colored flowers may appear too "contrasty" because of the strength and variety of the colors used. The contrast can be reduced and the color scheme rendered more harmonious by adding very small amounts of the colors of each flower into the green of its leaves. This is called "graying" and is very effective especially when the color is left in streaks rather than thoroughly mixed into the green.

In general avoid deep colors except for small areas (accents) and perhaps in Christmas and Halloween cakes. Follow nature in choosing color schemes and allow your creative imagination to guide you.

THE IMPORTANCE OF COLOR TECHNIQUE IN MODERN CAKE DECORATING

Knowledge of the proper color techniques will help you in obtaining natural coloring, dramatic effects, unusual combinations and in general will help make your decorated cakes look more beautiful, colorful and outstanding.

The 6 techniques described here will serve as a guide and an outline to which you will undoubtedly add your own techniques as you become more familiar and accomplished in the coloring of your own decorated pieces.

SPATULA STRIPING

This is the most usual color blending method. After placing a tube in the cone, use a small bow knife and put a one inch strip of colored icing down the entire side of the cone. After striping the cone, fill the remainder of the cone with white icing. As an example, let's say you want to make some pink and white roses. The pink will appear on the inside of the rose and the white should be out at the tips. This simulates the way nature bleaches out the rose at the tips of the petals. In this case you would strip the large side of a No. 104 tube in pink icing with a strip approximately ½ inch thick and 1 inch wide and the remainder would be filled with white icing. Then as you make your rose, the petals will be pink except for the tips which are white.

This method of striping can and should be used on borders. In making a shell border with a large star tube, the cone should have a narrow strip of colored icing on one side. The rest of the cone is filled with white icing. This gives the border a beautiful two-tone effect.

DEEP COLOR METHOD

For all decorators the problem of getting a deep red or green is almost an impossibility. By using the brush method of striping, this becomes relatively simple. First make up some medium colored icing. Place paste color on brush, and swab it around the entire inside of the cone. After this is completed, fill your cone with the colored icing. With this method all of the coloring is on the outside of the flower or border and is not wasted on the inner part.

This method can be used for many different occasions and is not only practical but makes your colors go much further.

MASKING METHODS

This method, illustrated on the opposite page in the winter scene cake, is a technique similar to the use of a stencil. The desired pattern or figure is cut out of a piece of heavy cardboard. This mask can then be used over and over again. The icing may be applied with a spatula to the cake areas not covered by the mask, or colored areas may be sprayed on.

In the illustrated cake, a separate mask was used for the sky, mountains and evergreens. In producing a large number of cakes with the same design, use one on all cakes successively and then go over the cakes with the other masks in turn. After the icing or coloring has been applied by the masking method, further decoration may be accomplished by piping.

COLOR STRIPING

This is a new idea in striping your cone with many different colors and still using a plain white icing.

For a fall leaf effect, strip the cone in 3 places. First with brown coloring on each side, then with green in the middle. These strips should be about ⅛ of an inch wide and extend from top to bottom of the cone. After striping is completed, the cone is filled with pastel green icing. The leaves will have a beautiful three tone effect; a pastel green leaf with brown on each side and a deep green shade in the center. All of this is done simply by making 3 strips.

SPRAYING METHOD

The spraying method of coloring is becoming more popular every day. In using this method, no expensive equipment is necessary. It will cost you just 20c for an atomizer at any Art store. With this simple atomizer, all of your spraying equipment is taken care of.

The flowers are made up first on wax paper in white icing. Then take a small glass of water and color it delicately with paste color. The flowers are then sprayed with the colored water with the atomizer. These flowers must be made up and sprayed before placing them on a cake. Very deep colors may be attained by simply making your water a dark color.

BLENDING PULLED SUGAR

Fall leaves, the orchid and similar decorations in pulled sugar require two or more colors. The blending of the colors is easily achieved. As an example, consider the fall leaf: A one inch strip of yellow candy is placed on top of a piece of green candy three inches in diameter. The leaf is then pulled out as described in detail under *Pulled Sugar*. As the leaf is formed, the two colors blend giving the desired effect. Another small piece of candy in a third color may be added to create pulled sugar in three blended colors.

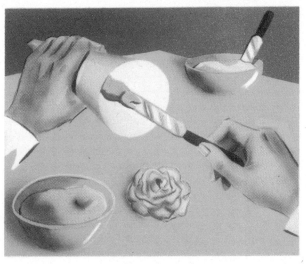

SPATULA STRIPING

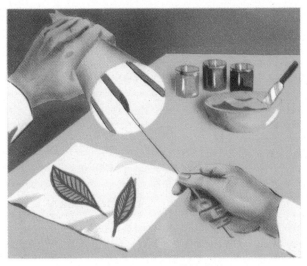

BRUSH STRIPING

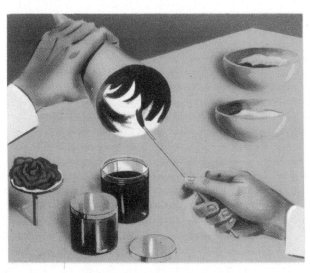

DEEP COLOR METHOD

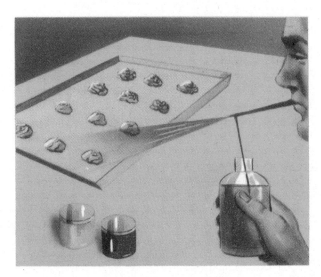

SPRAYING METHOD

MASKING METHOD

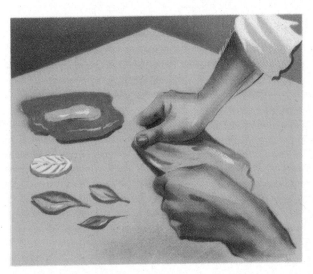

BLENDING PULLED SUGAR

CHAPTER II

Cake Borders

It is hoped that the reader will at least try all of the borders shown on these pages.
Once you have tried them, you will see that they are not complicated or
difficult and are not even very time consuming. You may believe that for the large variety
of borders shown here, you will need a great many tubes.
The majority of the borders shown on these pages require only three tubes.
The basic decoration of most cakes is the border. Aside from the attractiveness of the borders
themselves, they perform the functions of smoothing the cake edges, covering
flaws and cracks and giving the cake a uniform appearance.

TOP BORDER

Most top borders are put on the cake at about a 45 degree angle as illustrated. We do this for two reasons. It covers the edges or corners of the cake and also gives the border a more attractive appearance.

SIDE BORDER

This illustrates working on the side of a cake. The cone should be held in a comfortable position. On most side borders the tube is held off to the side of the cake. Using this cone position, the icing will flow in a smooth and even pattern.

TOP AND SIDE BORDER

In this illustration we are using a string border which is worked around the base of a top border. The tube is held off at a slight angle. In any combination of top and side borders, the top border is piped on first.

BOTTOM BORDER

A bottom border is worked around the base of a cake or cake tier and is normally piped on at a 45 degree angle to the cake. If the border is piped on perpendicular to the base it gives the border an unfinished appearance.

FUNDAMENTALS

The only way to become proficient at making these borders is to practice them on a cake pan. Any of our decorating icings may be used for all of these borders. After completing several of the borders, your pan may be scraped off with a spatula knife and the icing returned to your bowl to be used for more practice border work. As in all cake decorating, border work requires even pressure control along with smooth co-ordinated movements. With proper pressure and movement of the cone, almost any design can be made. Neatness and uniform-

ity of design are essential. Master these and your borders will become a series of simple steps that you can execute swiftly and with precision. Make a batch of icing, using one of our decorating icing recipes. Place a damp cloth over the icing to keep it from crusting. Use a cake pan or a similar hard top surface to practice your borders on. Construct a large cone and place a tube in the cone and fill the cone about half full of icing. Fold the cone over and roll slightly to keep the icing from backing out the wrong end.

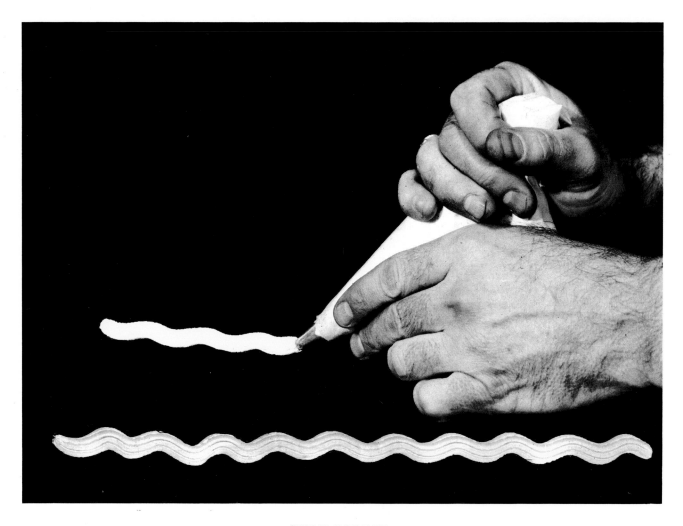

SWAY BORDER

Using the No. 30 star tube, the cone should be held at a 45 degree angle to the surface as illustrated. In squeezing the cone remember that the pressure is applied with the entire right hand. The left hand is used as a guide.

Rest the tube lightly on the pan and start moving along with a gentle side to side motion while continuing a steady even pressure on the tube. This is the only movement required to complete this border.

ZIG-ZAG BORDER

Using a No. 30 tube, the cone is held at a 45 degree angle to the surface. Rest the tube lightly on the pan for practice. Start an even steady pressure on the cone and as you move along, the cone is moved in a short side to side motion.

LOOP BORDER

 A No. 30 tube is used to construct this border and is held at a 45 degree angle. As pressure is applied to the cone, the tube is moved along resting lightly on the pan at all times. As you move along a series of slight oval movements should be maintained. This creates a fluted effect.

NARROW ZIG-ZAG BORDER

A No. 16 star tube is used for this border. The cone is held at a 45 degree angle. The tube should be touching the pan at all times. As you move the tube along, continue a steady side to side motion using an even pressure on the cone at all times. If the border builds up too much it is because you are using too much pressure. If your icing breaks you are not applying enough pressure to the cone.

STAR FLOWER BORDER

A No. 30 star tube is used for this border. The cone is held perpendicular to the pan. Apply pressure, stop squeezing and pull away from the pan. This will break the border off and give you the small star effect. Using a series of these motions in a straight line completes this border.

DROP FLOWER BORDER

Using a No. 30 star tube, fill a cone half full of icing. Hold the cone perpendicular to the pan for practice. Start applying gentle pressure, move away from the pan in a circular motion. While pressure is being applied and while using a circular motion, lift the tube approximately ¼ inch from the pan. Discontinue pressure and continue the circular motion. This will break the border off neatly.

CURLYCUE BORDER

A No. 16 tube is used for this border. The cone is held at a 45 degree angle and should touch the pan slightly at all times. With a gentle side to side motion the tube is moved along while a steady pressure is maintained. After this is completed, using the same tube, the small curlycues are placed in by starting off to the side, lightly squeezing, relaxing pressure and moving into the original line. This border may be worked around the side of the cake. When working around the side of the cake, it should be elevated to approximately eye level.

FLAT BORDER

A No. 67 leaf tube is used for this border. For practice, the cone is held at a 45 degree angle to the pan with the surface of the tube being held flat on the pan. Start a steady even pressure and move the tube slightly in a side to side motion as the cone is moved along the pan's surface.

SERRATED FLAT BORDER

A No. 67 leaf tube is used for this border. The cone is held at a 45 degree angle to the pan with the surface of the tube in a flat position on the pan. As pressure is applied, move the tube forward and backward continuing a steady even pressure with your right hand.

FLUTED EDGE BORDER

A No. 67 leaf tube is used for this border. The tube is held at a 45 degree angle to the pan. Instead of holding the tube flat to the surface, it is placed up on its side. Start an even pressure and move the tube along with a series of slight up and down motions. The more variation in the back and forth motion the larger the fluted edge will be.

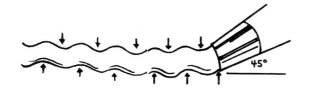

PLAIN FLAT BORDER

A No. 104 tube is used for this border. The opening of the tube should be held flat to the surface of the pan. The cone is held at a 45 degree angle. The tube is moved in a side to side motion with a steady even pressure giving this border a ribbon effect.

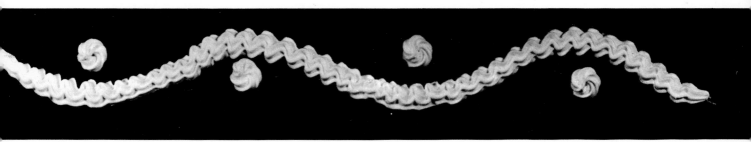

RIBBON BORDER

A No. 104 tube is used for this border. The surface of the tube is held flat to the pan. With a steady even pressure the cone is moved from side to side in a series of quick movements while pressure is applied to the cone.

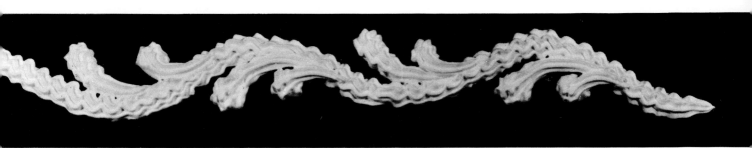

ROSETTE BORDER

A No. 16 star tube is used for this border. This border is to be worked on the side of the cake but may be practiced on a flat pan. The cone is held at a 45 degree angle. As pressure is applied the cone is moved in a series of quick side to side motions as a slight up and down pattern is formed. At each curve of the border a small rosette is added.

SIDE SCROLL BORDER

This is a border for the side of a cake. For practice you may work on a pan. A No. 16 star tube is used for this border. The cone is held at a 45 degree angle to the surface. With a series of side to side movements, a slightly curved pattern is followed. After this is completed two small curves are worked into each large curve of the border. This is done using the same tube and applying pressure and working down into your border. As you reach the border, relax pressure, discontinue squeezing and move on into the border. This breaks the icing off in a smooth even pattern.

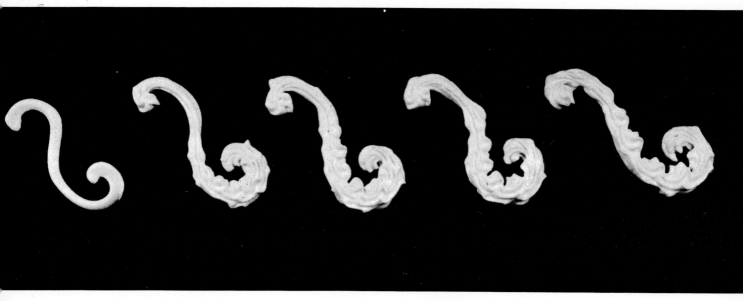

DAINTY SIDE SCROLL BORDER

A No. 16 star tube is used for this border. It is to be used on the side of a cake but may be practiced on the flat surface of a pan. The tube is held at a 45 degree angle to the surface. A slight back and forth movement is maintained while following the elongated curved design. After completing this, the smaller curves are worked into the design by starting off to the side, squeezing hard and turning the tube slightly as you come down into the original design.

SEPARATED BORDER

A No. 16 star tube was used for this design. This design is for the side of a cake but may be practiced on the flat surface of a pan. With the tube touching the cake slightly at all times, the design is first piped on. Using the same tube, start at the bottom of the design in a circular clock-wise motion and follow the design around relaxing pressure then drawing straight around to the other curl completing the feather effect.

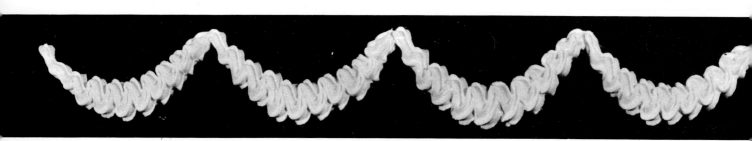

DRAPED RIBBON BORDER

A No. 16 tube is used for this border. This border is for the side of a cake but may be practiced on a flat surface if desired. Start a light pressure moving the tube slightly in an up and down motion. As the tube moves down to the middle of the drop, the pressure is increased slightly along with your back and forth movement. As the tube is brought up to the finish of the design, the pressure is decreased along with the back and forth motion.

SHELL BORDER

Just as the name implies, this is a series of shells connected together in a continuous line. Use a No. 30 Star Tube. Hold the cone at a 60 degree angle to the cake's surface. Begin squeezing. As the shell builds up raise the tube about ¼ inch . . . then ease off on your pressure as you pull down. The shell comes down to a point by stopping all pressure at the end of the shell.

SHELL BORDER WITH RUFFLED OUTER EDGE

After the shell border described above is completed, use a No. 3 tube to make the outer edge. This is done with a series of back and forth movements while continuing an even pressure on the cone. This outer edge is normally in a contrasting color.

RIBBON SHELL BORDER

Upon completing the shell border, use a No. 104 tube for the outer border. The tube is held at a 10 degree angle to the surface with the heavy end of the tube touching the shell . . . and the narrow end standing out. By applying an even pressure and moving your tube along, a ribbon edge is obtained. To get each ribbon edge to break off properly, you must relax pressure and finally stop squeezing altogether when you come to the end of each shell.

To complete the left side of the Ribbon Shell, hold the tube in the same manner but swing your hand over to the other side of the shell to a 10 degree angle from the surface and follow the same procedure as above.

REVERSE SHELL BORDER

This border is similar to the plain Shell Border except that as the shell is built up, you circle to the right and ease off the pressure. The second shell is circled to the left and so on.

ROPE BORDER

The Rope Border is almost self-explanatory. A No. 30 star tube was used for this border, but any size may be used. The first step is to make a slight S with the Star Tube. The second S is started at the lower left side of the first S giving the border a rope effect.

BULB BORDER

This is made in the same manner as the Shell Border using a cone cut to a ¼ inch opening. Finish it off with an outer edge and a small double drop string border using a No. 3 tube.

FRENCH PLUME BORDER

Use a large Star tube to make the star-like drops. Make them close together. Pipe a three-quarter circle around the top of the star with a No. 16 tube. Overpipe the three-quarter circle using a No. 3 tube. Then place the leaves on with the use of a No. 67 Leaf tube.

ALTERNATING PLUME BORDER

Use a No. 16 Star tube for the alternating curves. The pressure must be diminished at the end of each plume. Use the same tube and go over the plumes applying very little pressure. The entire border is then overpiped with a No. 3 tube using a contrasting color.

STAR DROP BORDER

Use a No. 199 tube for the Star drops. Hold the tube perpendicular to the cake and 1/16 of an inch up. By merely squeezing—then relaxing pressure the star is formed. Use a small Star tube for the outer edge and overpipe this with a No. 3 tube. A very fine cone is used to make the small circle in the middle of the star.

SHELL BORDER WITH FLUTED EDGE

This border is normally used around the base of a wedding cake. The shell is made with a No. 199 tube. The fluted edge is made with a No. 104 tube in the same manner as the outer edge described in the Star Drop Border. The difference is in the ruffles of the edge, which is accomplished by a slight back and forth motion as you move your tube along. The lower, outer edge is self-explanatory. A contrasting color should be used for the fluted edge.

SHELL BORDER WITH "S" SCROLL

After completing the shell, the "S" border is put on with a No. 3 tube. Use a contrasting color. By taking a close look you will see that the "S" is started at the front of the shell and passes across and back to the second shell. Notice carefully where the second "S" is started. This border is completed with the "S" Scroll. If you care to go into more detail; you may do so as shown above.

A FEW WORDS ABOUT STRING WORK

Before we go on to the next group of borders we want to give you a few hints on STRING WORK. This type of border is frequently referred to as being difficult. This, we can assure you, is not the case. Actually string work is easy. The most important thing about String Work is to use the proper icing . . . Royal or Boiled, thinned down to the proper consistency. If your icing is too thin or soft it will not hold together. If it is too stiff it will not string out or flow smoothly. It must be just right.

For practice we suggest that you work on the sides of a cookie pan or similar object, that is in an upright position.

Once you have mastered the first drop border the rest will become an effortless movement of repetition. Each string drops slightly below the other in a smooth exactness as though it were put on by machine.

For all of the following string work use a small cone with a No. 3 tip filled with slightly thinned-down boiled icing.

SINGLE DROP BORDER

Practice on upright pan. Use the top of your pan as a guide line. Touch the pan with the tip of your tube and start squeezing with an even pressure. Do not move your cone down over the drop. Let gravity pull your string down. Move your string over about 1½ inches as you squeeze and let the strings drop about one inch. Your hand should be at the top of the pan at all times. If you follow the drop down with your tube it is impossible to get uniform string work, especially in the longer string work.

EXTENDED DROP BORDER

Hold the No. 3 tube perpendicular to the pan. A small point is built up by a steady pressure on the cone. After the point is built up, move the tube away from the pan. Continue with an even pressure and let the string drop down in the same manner as described in the above border. The next mound, or point, is started right in the center of the first drop. Follow this procedure around the entire cake. This Extended Border should stand out approximately ½ inch from the side of your pan or cake. For this border to extend properly, the icing should be a little stiffer than for your normal string work.

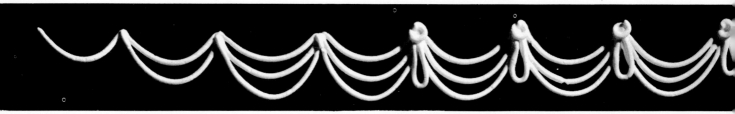

STRING QUADRUPLICATE BORDER

This drop border is spaced about two inches apart. Steps 1, 2, and 3 (beginning at the left of the illustration) show the procedure of dropping each string slightly below the other. Note, each string starts and finishes at the same point. A small drop is placed between each of the connecting points and then a circle on top.

TRIPLE DROP BORDER

Start this border in the same manner as the string Quadruplicate Border. The second three drops are started in the middle of the first one. The third three drops are started directly on the end of your first as shown in the fourth step on the above illustration.

STRING QUINTET BORDER

Each drop is started directly below the other. The smallest, which is the center, is dropped first. Note—the other two strings *do not* start or finish as in the above border. After completing the first three drops, start the second series by dropping the small string first. Notice this small string is started by attaching it to the last and longest string of the first series. The No. 2 string is connected to the center string of the first series and so on. Steps 3 and 4 illustrate the other two strings that are draped in to complete the String Quintet.

DOUBLE DROP BORDER WITH BOW

The above illustration is self-explanatory except for the bow. When piping the bow, make a figure 8 with your cone.

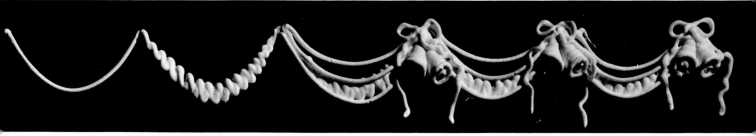

WEDDING BELL BORDER

Use a No. 3 tube to complete this entire border. After dividing off the cake as shown in step one, go over the string by moving the cone in an up and down motion while following the guide line. The three strings are then dropped over this line. Pipe in the bells by using a light pressure and increasing the pressure as you move to outer edge of the bell. Finish off with a small bow on top of the bells.

CURVED GARLAND BORDER

Drop in the guide line first. Go over the guide line with a No. 16 Star tube. Place on the Leaf at the point where the borders connect. Use a No. 3 tube to finish off the border at the top. This border may also be used to go around the top of the cake instead of the side as illustrated on our Christmas Cake Tops.

RIBBON BORDER

Use a No. 104 tube to complete this border. The large end of the tube touches the cake—the small end stands out slightly. If too much pressure is applied to the cone the ribbon will be rippled instead of smooth. This border may be used for either the side or the top of a cake, as you desire.

COLONIAL SCROLL BORDER

This border is normally used on the side of a cake. First, make an outline around the entire cake as shown in the first two sections. Glide your tube over the pan or cake icing with a light, even motion. Go over these lines using the same tube. You obtain the Feather effect by making small circular counter-clockwise movements while applying steady pressure on the cone.

REVERSE SCROLL BORDER

This differs from the above border in that each curve goes in an opposite direction. It is finished off in the same manner except for the curve that goes up. When putting the feather effect on this curve, you must move the cone in a small series of clockwise circular motions.

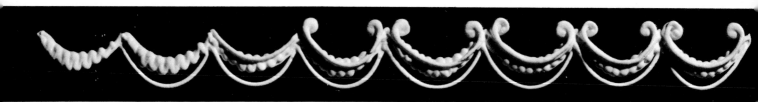

DROPPED GARLAND BORDER

This is another border that may be used for either the side or the outer edge of the cake top. Use a No. 3 tube to complete the entire border. Use the techniques explained previously in this section of the book, and follow the steps 1 to 4 shown above.

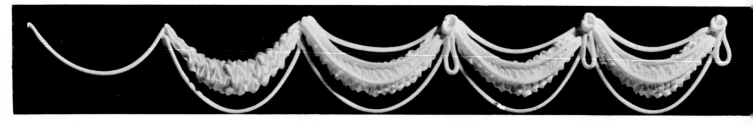

DROPPED CRESCENT—SIDE BORDER

First, drop a guide line around the cake approximately 2½ inches in width and 1½ inches down as shown in step 1. Go over this line with a No. 16 Star tube. Note the start of this border is small. As it moves down it becomes wider, as it comes back up, it diminishes again. This is accomplished by easing off and applying pressure. Next, a single drop line is placed under each crescent. Then three smaller drop lines are worked above this line. Make a small drop line and a tiny bell-like circle where the crescents meet. All drop line work is completed with a No. 3 tube.

DRAPED GARLAND WITH FLUTED EDGE

Using a No. 3 tube a guide line is first dropped around the entire cake, as shown in step No. 1. Then using a No. 104 tube, the fluted edge is finished in the following manner: The heavy end of the tube touches the guide line, the small end stands out and down. Using an even pressure on the cone, move the tube in a up and down motion along the guide line. After this is completed the border is then finished off in the same manner as the Dropped Crescent-Side Border. We suggest that you practice the fluted edge on the side of an upright pan a few times before attempting to put this border on your cake.

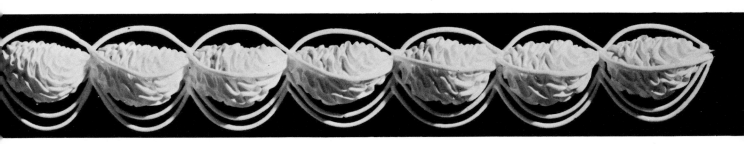

FULL GARLAND

Using a No. 30 star tube fill a large cone with white icing. Practice this border a few times on the side of an upright pan before attempting to place it on the cake. Hold the tube perpendicular to the side of your cake. Using a constant pressure, move the tube slowly away from the cake as the icing builds up, start back to the cake and diminish your pressure. Notice this garland border starts small, is built out heavy, and then goes back to the cake small again. When you start the second garland, you will have a tendency to crowd it against the first one. Your pressure must be started again very lightly. Move away from the side of the cake, build up the pressure, relax pressure and return to the cake. Continue this garland around the entire cake. After this is completed, the double dropped string work is put on using a No. 3 tube.

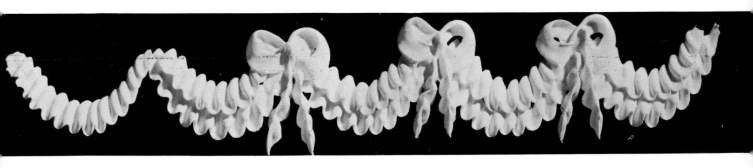

RIBBONETTE BORDER

This border is completed entirely with a No. 104 tube. If you desire, you may strip the tube on the narrow side with a pastel colored icing and fill the remainder of the tube with white icing. The heavy end of the tube touches the cake; the small end stands out and down. Using a uniform pressure move the tube in an up and down motion as shown in step No. 1. After completing this movement around the entire cake, the second ribbonette is worked on in exactly the same manner slightly above the first one. The next step is to complete the bows. To complete this bow, your tube must be touching the cake slightly at all times. With a constant pressure on the cone, make a figure eight moving the cone very slowly. This completes the bow. Place your tube at the center of the bow and come down with the strings. If your bow has a tendency to fold up it is because your tube is not touching the side of the cake.

RIBBON SWAG BORDER

The No. 104 tube is used for this border. The large end of the tube touches the cake and the small end faces up and slightly out. With a steady, even pressure, move the cone along the side of the cake. The large end of the tube must be touching the cake at all times. Make the top part of the ribbon first. The lower portion is completed next. If the ribbon ruffles, too much pressure is being applied to your cone. The small ribbon is made with a No. 3 tube. This must be touching the cake slightly at all times to maintain the proper shape of the bow.

ROPE VARIATION BORDER

Use the same procedure as described in the Rope Border but with a No. 199 tube. This is a much heavier border and is always used as the base of a cake or the lower portion of the wedding cake.

REVERSE VARIATION BORDER

In completing this border a No. 199 tube is used. After building up the shell, relax pressure and move in a circular motion slightly to the right. Relax your pressure completely at the bottom. The same procedure is followed for the next reverse except that after the shell is built up, you move to the left in a circular motion. This border is heavier than usual and should be used only on larger cakes.

LILY OF THE VALLEY BORDER

A delicate green is first piped around the side of your cake using a No. 3 tube. The long narrow leaves are made with a small cone of green icing cut to shape a leaf. These leaves should be brought off from the inside of each curve of the stem giving the border a more uniform look. The small white lilies are piped on with a small cone using a No. 3 tube. Each is made to simulate a tiny bell. This border may be used on the upper tiers of your wedding cake.

ROSE BORDER

A delicate green stem is first piped around the side of your cake using a No. 3 tube. The leaves are then piped on using a No. 67 leaf tube also in the delicate green color. The rose buds and the dainty roses should be made up ahead of time and put on after drying. This is used normally on large anniversary or wedding cakes.

SHELL VARIATION BORDER

The shell border was made with a No. 199 tube. This border is fairly large or heavy and should be used around the base of your decorated cakes. The fluted edge on the bottom portion of the border is done with a No. 104 tube stripped with a delicate color on the narrow side. The heavy end of the tube touches the border. The small end stands out slightly. With a continuous pressure move the tube along the shell using a slight back and forth motion in your movement. This gives the ruffled affect. The upper portion of the shell is finished off with a No. 3 tube. Make a series of back and forth motions following the curve of the shell to complete the edging of the border.

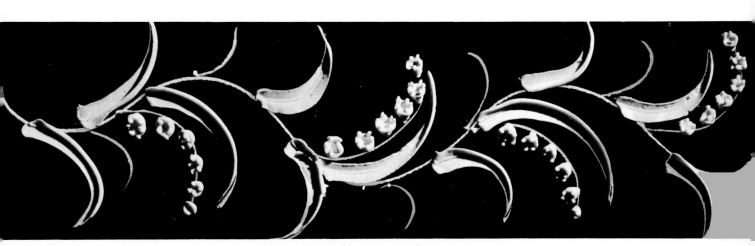

LILY OF THE VALLEY VARIATION BORDER

This is made in almost the same manner as the Lily of the Valley Border. It is a little more complicated and is placed on the side of a cake where you have more area to work in. The leaves are put on with the use of a No. 67 leaf tube. Instead of putting the lilies directly on the leaves as we did before we first draw a fine stem from the vine. The lilies are then piped on the stems.

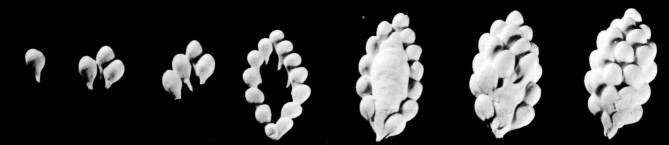

THE GRAPEVINE BORDER

This border may be used for either wedding or holiday cakes. When used on a wedding cake complete the entire border in white icing. We shall describe it in color. Using a No. 3 tube filled with thinned down purple icing, practice making a bunch of grapes on a flat surface. The grapes are a series of small shells as shown in steps 1 to 3. These shells are made in the same manner as the shell border except they are very tiny. The tube is held at a 45 degree angle to begin. Applying pressure, lift the tube up slightly, then ease off on the pressure and return back to your pan or whatever you happen to be working on.

Continue this procedure until an outline of a bunch of grapes is formed, as shown in step 4. The center is then filled as in step 5. Now continue your grapes on this built-up mound until the entire bunch is completed. After practicing a few bunches of grapes, draw a long curved line to simulate the stems. The bunches of grapes are placed on the inside of the curves. The leaves are green and brown and are made in colors by using the brush method as described in Color Techniques. The leaves are made in a series of threes. The small curled twigs or climbers are then put on completing the border as shown above.

FLORAL VINE BORDER

This is another border for the side of a cake and may be used on either wedding or birthday cakes. The procedure followed is much like the two borders just described. The dainty flowers shown here are drop flowers and are pictured in detail in the floral section.

The flowers are made up beforehand with royal icing. After the vine is made, the leaves are piped on. The drop flowers are placed on by piping a small spot of icing under each flower and placing it in position.

HOLLY BORDER

This is a Christmas border to be completed in deep colors obtained by the brush method described in Color Techniques. The vine is first piped on in deep green working around the cake in a curved graceful line. The holly leaves described under Leaves are piped on from either side with a No. 67 leaf tube filled with a slightly thinned down green icing. Red holly berries are placed on at various intervals completing border.

THE ROSEBUD BORDER

This border is completed in the same manner as the Holly Border except all the colors are pastel. The leaves are put on using the No. 67 leaf tube. They are made very small by using light pressure as you bring the leaf out. The rosebuds are made up ahead of time and placed on a little mound of icing after drying. These buds may be made right on the side of the cake, but it is much faster to make them up ahead of time and attach them after drying.

THE FLOWERED GARLAND BORDER

This is a very lovely border used on the side of a wedding cake. Tiny orange blossoms are made up in advance. After a guide line is placed around your cake, the blossoms are put on using a small mound of icing under each flower. A few delicate green leaves and a bow on top finishes off this unusual border.

49

CHAPTER III

Flowers

Flower making is actually fun. The simplest little bud, will give you
a real feeling of accomplishment. The more you practice the
greater degree of perfection you will obtain. Each time you make a new flower
strive for a little more perfection than the last. This way you will soon master the
art of flower making.

Our primary aim in selecting the flowers for this chapter is to give you the
fundamental steps that are the basis for all flowers. These flowers are the most
practical to use. They can be made in a minimum of time using production line
methods and with the least number of tubes, nails, etc.

As you progress from one flower to another you will see that our methods make
each step as effortless as possible.

ELEMENTARY STEPS IN FLOWER DESIGNS

The first twelve flowers that we describe are simple to make. All of these flowers with the exception of two will be made with a nail and tube used together. For the first few flowers you may have difficulty in controlling the pressure and at the same time turning the nail with the left hand. Remember that the nail is turned in a counter-clockwise direction. As we progress with our flower making series, it will be necessary to turn the nail and squeeze out the petal in a co-ordinated movement. You will have a tendency to apply pressure on your cone and then turn your nail. We suggest that you practice holding the nail in your left hand and slowly turning it around and around in an easy continuous movement.

For the first three flowers you will need the No. 30 star tube in a large cone. To put these flowers directly on a cake you may use any type of icing you desire. If these flowers are to be made up in advance, a royal icing must be used in order that the flowers will dry and may be placed on the cakes later.

We will practice these flowers on a sheet of waxed paper that has been fastened down with a small amount of icing on an inverted cookie pan.

This illustrates the proper angle of the tube when constructing the first three simple flowers.

Holding the tube at right angles to the pan, touch the waxed paper and squeeze lightly; relax pressure completely and lift up. Make a complete row along the pan using the same procedure. It is simply squeeze, relax and lift away to form a tiny flower.

Using No. 30 tube and also the same position, touch the waxed paper, apply pressure, continue applying pressure until the flower enlarges. Discontinue pressure and lift away. Using this same tube a slightly larger flower is formed.

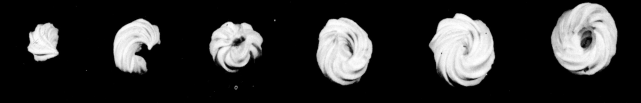

THE ROSETTE

Still working on the waxed paper and holding the tube at right angles to your pan as illustrated, start with a light pressure and, turning in a counter-clockwise motion, continue pressure and turn until you return to the starting point. Relax pressure at this point, stop squeezing and continue turning in the same direction. The icing will break off neatly and the rosette will be formed.

For the next eight flowers we will use the nail and the tube together. This illustrates the proper way to hold the nail in relation to the cone. When making a very small flower on a nail it is necessary to use a royal icing. If a soft icing were used it would be impossible to remove the flower from the nail.

Drop a No. 16 star tube into a medium sized cone. Fill the cone with royal icing. Cut a few squares of waxed paper as illustrated. Place a dot of royal icing on the nail and fasten a square of waxed paper to the nail by pushing it into the dot of royal icing. We begin the first simple flower using both nail and tube.

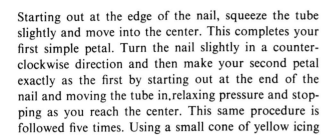

Starting out at the edge of the nail, squeeze the tube slightly and move into the center. This completes your first simple petal. Turn the nail slightly in a counter-clockwise direction and then make your second petal exactly as the first by starting out at the end of the nail and moving the tube in, relaxing pressure and stopping as you reach the center. This same procedure is followed five times. Using a small cone of yellow icing with a very small tip, make a yellow dot in the center of the flower for the stamen. After the flower is complete slide the waxed paper to the cookie pan and continue practicing a few of these flowers.

In about 12 hours these flowers will harden and may be gently peeled away from the waxed paper and used for decorating cupcakes and cookies.

In making this flower you will see that with the same tube and using a little more pressure a larger flower may be made. Starting out slightly further out on your waxed paper square, apply strong pressure, and as you move in, relax pressure and stop. This forms the first petal. Turn the nail slightly in a counter-clockwise direction. The second petal is made in the same manner working toward the center. This same procedure is followed 6 times. The center is piped on by making a yellow dot and continuing in a circular motion around the dot.

This flower will give you practice in co-ordinating pressure on the cone and the movement of the nail. Using your No.16 star tube, start at the outer edge of the nail. Touch the tube to the nail and apply pressure. As you move in to the center of the nail start a gradual turn with the nail in your left hand forming the petal as illustrated. The second petal is started in the same manner. Touch the outside of the nail and apply pressure. As you start moving toward the center with the tube, turn the nail slightly. This procedure is followed until six petals are formed. A small dot and circle is used for the center to give the flower a finished look.

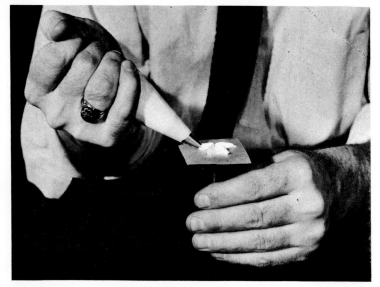

A No. 16 star tube is used in a cone filled with colored royal icing. A small square of waxed paper is fastened to the top of the nail. In making this flower a dot is placed in the center of the nail. The first petal is started directly in the center of the nail. Start squeezing; move out slowly ½ inch; relax pressure completely and continue moving your hand out. This will break the petal off to a point as illustrated. The nail is turned slightly. Again starting at the center of the nail, apply pressure holding the tube at the angle illustrated. Start squeezing, move out ½ inch, relax pressure completely and continue moving out. Again the petal will be broken off to a point. The nail is then moved and the same procedure is followed until six petals are formed.

During Christmas holidays, a very simple poinsettia may be made in this manner by using a deep red icing. After the flower is completed slide the waxed paper off the nail and place it on an inverted cookie pan.

No. 16 tube is used for this flower. A square of waxed paper is fastened to the nail and a small dot of icing is placed on the center of the waxed paper. The cone is held in the manner illustrated. The petal is started in the center of the nail. After applying pressure, move out slightly and turn the nail slightly as you are moving out. This will put a curve in the petal. The second petal is also started in the middle. A gentle pressure is applied to the cone. Move the cone out slightly and turn the nail at the same time. This procedure is followed until six petals are formed. Small yellow artificial stamens were placed in the center to give this flower a lifelike effect.

These stamens may be purchased in the dime store in the artificial flower section. Five or six stamens are cut from the bunch and put into the flower while the icing is still soft.

Use the No. 16 star tube. Fasten a small square of waxed paper to the nail. A round dot of icing is made in the center of the nail. This dot should be approximately ¼ inch in diameter as illustrated. Touch this dot on the outside with your tube, apply pressure, move away at a slight angle, relax pressure and continue moving. This will break your petal off to a point. This flower differs from the others: instead of keeping the tube flat on the nail you move out away from the nail. This movement will produce an erect petal on the nail. This same procedure is followed five times. After the flower is finished, small artificial stamens are cut and placed in the center of the flower.

SIMULATED DAISY

Fill a No. 16 star tube with white icing. Fasten a square of waxed paper on the nail and place a dot of icing in the center of the nail. Hold the tube as illustrated. Starting in the center of the nail, apply pressure and move out slightly while turning the nail. Relax pressure and continue moving, breaking the petal off at a point.

The second petal is then started in the center. Apply pressure, turn the nail slightly, move out, stop squeezing and continue moving the tube out again breaking the petal off to a point. This procedure is followed until about eight or ten are made. A dot of yellow icing is then piped in the center.

CHRYSANTHEMUM

To make the Mum, it is necessary to have your icing slightly thinner than normal. In order to break your petals off to a point, icing may be thinned down by adding a few drops of water and whipping. Use any colored icing to simulate the Mum. Place your No. 16 star tube in a cone and fill with icing. Fasten a square of waxed paper on the nail. Here we illustrate the procedure in building up a large dot in the center of the nail. This dot should be approximately ¾ inch in diameter and ½ inch high. This is done by holding the tube in the center of the nail, and with a continuous pressure as the dot builds out, move the tube about ½ inch up away from the nail. The first row of petals is started at the bottom of the large dot. Touch

the tube to the dot; squeeze; move away; relax pressure; stop squeezing completely and continue moving away. This breaks the petal off to a point. Continue this series of petals until the bottom row is filled. The same procedure is followed on the next row, but here the petals are made slightly shorter. After the second row is filled, start the third series of petals. This row should be drawn out and up instead of lying flat. After completing this row the center of the flower is then filled by drawing petals straight up and drawing these petals out to a point. When the flower is completed slide the waxed paper off the nail and place on an inverted cookie sheet.

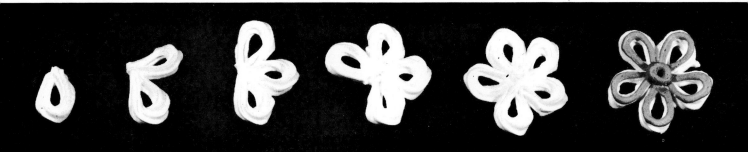

This flower is made with a No. 16 star tube in any desired icing. Place a piece of waxed paper on a nail. Starting in the center of your nail with the tube touching, move out in a circular motion and back to the starting point of origin thus completing your first petal.

Turn the nail slightly and start the second petal. This procedure is followed until five petals are made. Using a No. 4 tube and a contrasting color, go over these petals with a thin line as illustrated to complete this simplified flower.

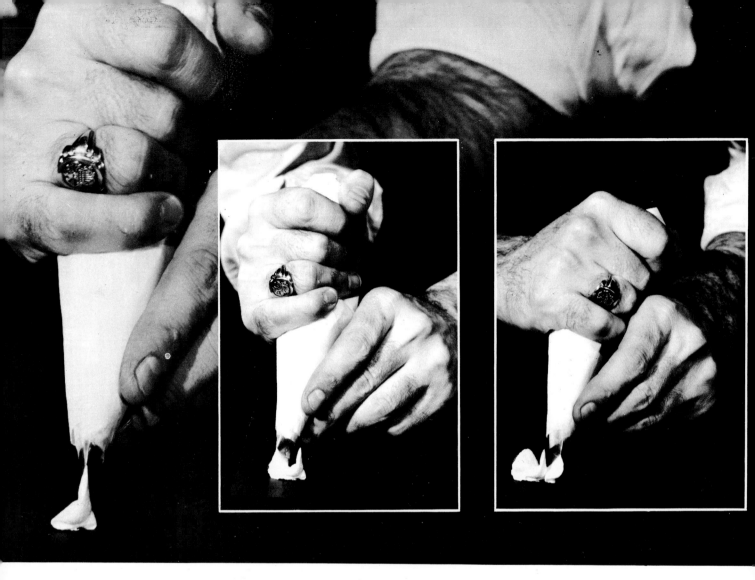

SWEETPEA

Here we illustrate the steps in making the Sweetpea. The tube is held at a 45 degree angle to the pan. With the heavy end of the tube touching the pan, apply pressure and lift the tube slightly. Continue squeezing, move the tube back to the starting point and discontinue squeezing forming the first petal. The second petal is started out with the tube angling out to the right. The heavy end of the tube touches the pan and the tube is lifted slightly. Continue pressure, move back down, relax pressure and stop as you come down to the starting point.

The third petal is started at the same point as the first but the tube is angled off to the left. Apply pressure and move the tube up while squeezing. Relax pressure as you come back down forming the sweetpea. See illustrated steps on next page.

This illustrates the proper position of the tube and cone when using the No. 104 tube for the apple blossom, petunia, briar rose, full carnation, pansy, yellow jonquil and wild rose. The heavy end of the tube is held down and the small end is angled up slightly to give a curved effect in the petals.

THE SWEETPEA

The simplest of all flowers to make is the sweetpea. Before attempting any of these flowers on a cake, we suggest that you practice them on a sheet of wax paper or the top of a cookie pan. Fill a No. 104 tube with any desired colored icing. The first step is to make the base as shown in figure 2. The heavy end of the tube should touch the pan, the small end stands out. Squeeze the cone and pivot the tube slightly to complete the base. The base is a flat lying-down petal. The first petal is then started directly in the center of the base. Again, with the narrow end of the tube up and the wide end touching the base, hold your cone at a 45 degree angle to the pan and start squeezing the cone and lifting the cone slightly. Then relax pressure and bring the tube down to the pan. At this point the pressure should be completely off the cone. This keeps the petal narrow. Too much pressure makes a wide and clumsy appearing petal. The second petal is started in the center again, but this time the tube is facing off to an angle. The same procedure is again followed for the next petal, making sure to come back to the center to finish the petal. The last petal is made in the same manner except that it is made on the opposite side of the center petal. The stems and leaves are put on using a small cone of green icing with a No. 3 tube.

ROSE BUD

Using a No. 104 rose tube and a small bow knife, put a one inch strip of pink icing on the entire side of the large end of the cone. Fill the remainder of the cone with white icing. For practice, rest the heavy end of the tube on the pan and the narrow end 3/16 of an inch off the pan. Turn the narrow end of the tube to the left about 10 degrees. Start squeezing and move the tube forward ¼ inch. With this movement, the first portion of the cup is formed as shown in figure 2. Straighten the tube out and ease off on pressure as the tube is moved back to the starting point. This will form the cup as shown in step 3. Now you want one more petal interlocking the first one as shown in step 5. Place the tube inside the cup. The large end of the tube should be touching the cup. Squeezing gently, lift the cone ⅜ of an inch up and then bring the petal over to the opposite side of the cup as shown in step 6. The bud is finished off with stem and leaves by the use of a small cone with a No. 3 tip filled with green icing.

DROP FLOWER

This is strictly a production flower and should be made up ahead of time on sheets of waxed paper using royal icing. By changing color and center, you can make three different types of flowers. Pink would be an apple blossom, white an orange blossom, and purple a violet. Using a No. 190 drop flower tube, fill a cone with royal icing. Stick a sheet of waxed paper to a pan.

Rest the tube on the waxed paper, holding the cone perpendicular to the pan. Turn the hand to the left as far as possible, then squeeze the cone and turn the hand to the right as far as possible while squeezing. This gives five distinct petals with just one operation. If the petals are too thick, too much pressure has been applied to the cone.

SMALL IMITATION DAISY

This is another production flower made up with a straight royal icing. Fill a No. 199 tube with white icing. Stick a sheet of waxed paper on a cookie pan. Rest the tube directly on the pan. The tube must be held perpendicular to the pan and completely motion-less. After applying pressure, relax pressure completely, lift the tube and the petals of the daisy are formed. Using a small cone filled with yellow icing and a No. 3 tip, the center is then piped in.

BACHELOR BUTTON

Fill a No. 30 star tube with white icing. Working on a sheet of waxed paper, rest the tube on the paper and squeeze. Relax pressure and lift the tube. The entire sheet of paper is filled with these large white dots as shown in step No. 1. Fill a small cone using a No. 3 tip with pink or blue icing, touch the tip to the center and squeeze, relax pressure and stop. Continue making these little points around the entire center as shown in Step 2, 3, and 4 until the center is completely full. This is a very simple flower you can complete to your satisfaction on the first try.

THE HALF ROSE

The half rose may be made up right on the cake or ahead of time. If made up ahead of time, a drying icing should be used. Fill a No. 104 tube with white icing or any desired color. The first step is to make the base. The base is made exactly as a sweet pea base as shown in flower No. 1, step 1. After the base is made the tube is held directly above the base, the small or narrow end of the tube stands out and the heavy end of the tube faces you. Squeeze the cone and lift up approximately ⅛ of an inch, relax pressure and lift the tube completely. This completes a simple bud that is made directly in the center of the base as shown in step 1. The next step is to place a petal over the left side of the bud. This is accomplished by holding the tube directly beside the bud and touching the base. Squeeze the tube and lift it up around the bud. Discontinue pressure and lift tube away completely. This will break off the petal. The same procedure is followed on the right side of the bud clinging as shown in step 3. The last two petals of the half rose must be standing out. This is accomplished in the following manner: With the heavy end of the tube touching the base of the bud and the small end standing out, start to squeeze and draw that petal up to the center of the bud, as shown in step 4. Stop squeezing and continue pulling the tube away. This will break the petal off. The petal on the right side, the last petal, is started in the same manner. The heavy end touches the base of the bud and the small end stands out. Starting at the very bottom of the bud, use pressure, move the tube up to the center of the bud, stop squeezing and continue moving. This will break the.petal off. The stem and the three small green stem-like leaves are made with a No. 3 tube with slightly thinned down green icing.

58

DAISY

The daisy must be made up in advance in royal icing and left to dry before placing on your cake top. For this flower you will need a No. 7 nail and a medium sized cone filled with royal icing. Use a No. 103 tube for the tip. Use the following method: Cut squares of waxed paper approximately 1½ inches wide, put a dot of royal icing on the nail and stick the waxed paper to it. After the flower is completed slide the waxed paper off onto a pan. Hundreds of flowers can be made with the use of one nail.

To start this flower, the nail is held with the left hand, using the thumb and forefingers to spin or revolve the nail. Put a dot of icing in the center of the nail and place the waxed paper on this dot. Before starting the flower, put a small dot of white icing in the center of the waxed paper. This will help you keep all your petals centered. With the large end of the tube touching the nail, start at the outer edge of the nail and squeeze while moving to the center of the nail and then ease off on the pressure to stop. Before attempting any more petals you should practice a few single petals. You will have a tendency to get a very heavy petal if you apply too much pressure. Figure No. 1 shows the approximate size of the first petal. After the first petal is made, the nail is turned and the procedure is followed until the flower is completed as shown in steps 1 to 7. The next step is to put the center in the daisy. This is accomplished by putting a large dot in the center with deep yellow icing. To give the daisy a lifelike effect, the center is then covered with yellow granulated sugar. Granulated sugar is colored by putting a small amount of paste color in the sugar and rubbing it in or mixing it in well with your hands. Moisten the tip of your finger, dip it in the yellow sugar and then touch the dot with your finger. This will deposit enough yellow sugar on the center and give the daisy a very lifelike look.

DAHLIA

To make the dahlia use a No. 103 tube and royal icing. Colors may be used as desired, red, yellow, white or a lovely deep purple. The cone should be stripped using the brush method that is described in *Color Techniques*. Stick a square of waxed paper on any flat nail. With the tube lying flat and slightly to the side, start the first petal from the outside of the nail easing off on the pressure until you come to the center as shown in Step 1. After this petal is completed, turn the nail slightly to finish the second petal. This procedure is repeated until the first row is finished. The second row is started about 1/16 of an inch from the first row. The narrow end of the tube is tipped up at a slight angle as shown in step 5. The last row is finished off in the same manner with the petals started slightly in from the following row and standing up a little higher—step 7. Yellow stamens are then placed in the center of the dahlia. The square of waxed paper is then slipped off the nail. These flowers must be made up ahead of time and allowed to dry.

APPLE BLOSSOM

This is another flower to be made in royal icing with the use of your No. 7 nail. Use a No. 104 tube filled with a delicate pink icing. Put a dot of icing on your nail and place the square of waxed paper on the nail. Tilt the cone in your right hand with the large end of the tube at a 45 degree angle directly in the center of the nail. As pressure is applied, move the tube out ⅛ of an inch turning the nail as the petal is being formed. See step 1. As you return to the starting point in making this first petal, ease off on the pressure and stop. Each petal is made in the same manner until five petals are formed, completing the apple blossom. The center is put in with a very fine tube. Slide the waxed paper off the nail and proceed with the next flower.

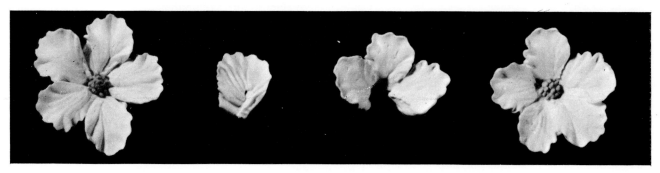

PETUNIA

A No. 104 tube is filled with a brilliant colored icing. A square of waxed paper is placed on a nail and the first petal is started at the center of the nail with the heavy end of the tube touching the nail and the small end standing out. As you apply pressure, start moving your tube out. With a slight back and forth motion, turn the nail slightly and bring the tube back to the center again. The back and forth motion produces the ruffled edge of the petal. Five petals are made in the same manner. Tiny bright yellow dots are used to complete the center of the petunia.

BRIAR ROSE

Because the petals are fairly large, the flower may be made up in buttercream, boiled or royal icing. Fill a large cone with icing using a No. 124 tube. A small mound of icing is first placed on the pan for practice. This is used as a base to work the petals around, shown in step one. With the heavy end of the tube touching the base and the small end standing out, apply light pressure. Now move the tube out approximately ⅛ of an inch, pivot the end of the tube slightly and come back to the starting point relaxing pressure as shown in step 2. The second petal is started directly beside the first. Apply pressure, move the tube out, pivot the narrow end of the tube, relax pressure and come back. This procedure is continued until five petals are completed. Tiny yellow stamens are then placed in the center of the flower.

HALF CARNATION

In order to create the desired effect of broken petal tips, it is necessary to use a very dry icing. To make your icing dry, simply add powdered sugar to the particular icing that you are using. Fill a No. 104 tube with pink or red icing. For practice hold the cone with the large end of the tube against the pan at an angle of 45 degrees. Squeeze the cone lifting slowly about ¼ inch off the surface, jiggling the cone as you squeeze to achieve the wavy effect and jagged edge. Upon reaching a height of ¼ of an inch, re-turn to the original position against the surface easing the pressure as you return. Repeat the operation outlined above making petals to the left and right as shown in figures 1, 2 and 3 until you have a fan of five or six petals. After completing the fan of petals, go through the same procedure, but this time work between and slightly above your first petals as shown in figures 5 and 6. This gives the flower a full rounded out effect.

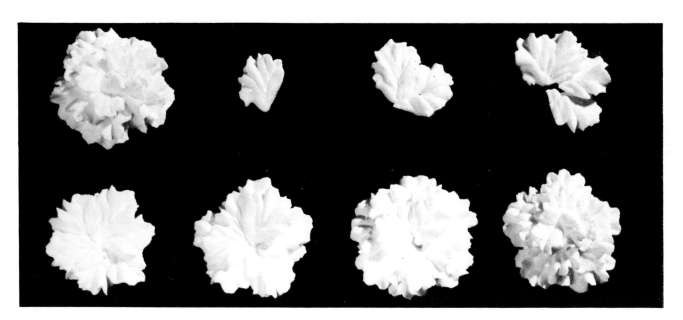

FULL CARNATION

To make the full carnation, the petals are made in the same way as for the half carnation illustrated above. The only difference is that the full carnation is made on a No. 7 nail. The nail is revolved in your fingers while each petal is being made. A complete circle of petals is made. Then the center of the car-nation is built up by filling up the spaces with the same type of petals until all spaces are filled, giving a full rounded effect. When making the full carna-tion for future use, cut 1½ inch squares of waxed paper and stick on the nail with icing as previously explained. After completing the carnation, slide the waxed paper onto the pan.

WILD ROSE

Use a No. 104 tube. Stick a square of wax paper on your No. 7 nail. The first row of petals is started around the outside of the nail as shown in steps 1 to 4. The second row is started in the center and is moved out approximately ⅛ of an inch from the tip of the first row as shown in step 5. The last row is made in the same manner starting in the very center and is slightly smaller than the second row. Yellow stamens are used to finish the wild rose.

POPPY

Fill a No. 104 tube cone with brilliant red icing. Stick a square of waxed paper on your No. 7 nail. Starting in the center of the nail, the heavy end of the tube is touching the nail with the small end standing out. Move the tube out about ¼ of an inch with a series of sharp back and forth motions. Turn the nail slightly and come back with the tube, relaxing pressure. These back and forth motions give the poppy a fluted effect. This same procedure is followed in making the four large petals. Starting at the very middle of the first four petals, three more petals are made in the same manner. To give the poppy a life-like effect, insert a bunch of black tipped paper stamens. There are two types of poppies—the 7 or 4 petaled flower. Make whichever you desire.

PANSY

Insert a No. 104 tube in a medium sized cone. Using the brush method, dip a brush into the purple paste color. Make a ¼ inch strip on the heavy side of the tube, and then, using the same method, dip the brush into the yellow paste coloring and put a ¼ inch strip up the narrow side of the tube. With a piece of waxed paper on your No. 7 nail start your first petal. The petal is started from the center of the nail. As you squeeze and move out, a slight back and forth motion is maintained to give the petal a ruffled edge. Three large petals are placed in this manner as shown in step 3. For the next row of petals, start in between any two petals of the first row. Start your petal from the middle and as you move out continue the back and forth motion, turn the nail, relax pressure and come back. One more large petal at the top is completed in the same manner, and then, if you wish, you may paint a little face in the center. The pansy can be made in many variations of brilliant colors.

YELLOW JONQUIL

This flower is made with the No. 104 tube filled with brilliant yellow icing. A 2 inch square of waxed paper is stuck to your No. 7 nail. The petal is started directly in the middle of the nail. With an easy pressure, start moving the tube out to the end of the nail. Upon reaching the end of the nail, turn the nail slightly. This turning motion gives the proper width to your petal. Stop the turning motion and continue back to the center relaxing pressure as you go. In starting the second petal as shown in figure 2, be sure not to crowd this petal too close to the first one. Each petal is separate and is not pushed or crowded to the previous petal. When the six petals are made as shown in figure 6, after dipping your fingers into cornstarch the tips of the petals may be pinched to give them the pointed effect. The center of the jonquil is finished off with a small cone of deep yellow using a No. 3 tube for the tip. This is a bell-like center. It is completed by touching the tube to the center of the flower, applying pressure, and, as you move up, continue to apply pressure and let the center build up into a bell shape. This should be built up approximately ½ inch high. At the top of the bell-like center, move the tube in an up and down motion as you turn your nail. This will give the center a ruffled edge effect. Upon completing the flower, slide the waxpaper off the nail onto a pan and let the flower dry.

CALLA LILY

The calla lily may be made with buttercream directly on the cake or may be made up ahead of time with royal icing to dry for future use. Using a No. 124 tube with white icing, start a slight curve with the tube squeezing as you move along. The heavy end should be touching the pan for practice and the narrow end standing up slightly.

The first step is a slight curve approximately 2 inches long as shown in step 1. As you come to the top of the calla lily, you will encounter difficulty in pivoting the tube around the point and following the curve back down as shown in step 2. Coming down again, be sure to keep the tube right next to the upward stroke. This will eliminate an opening in the flower. A green stem and leaf are then piped on with a small cone, using a No. 67 tube for the leaf and a No. 3 tube for the stem. The yellow stamen in the center is piped on in yellow icing with a No. 3 tube.

POINSETTIA

To make the poinsettia the inside of the cone is brushed with a red paste color and the cone is filled with red icing. If the flowers are to be made in advance, a royal icing should be used. The advantage in making these flowers up in advance is that they can be made on a nail much faster than on the cake. Also, in placing the royal icing on your cake, the flowers may be tipped on the side giving a more lifelike effect. If you use a nail, cut 2 inch squares of waxed paper and stick them on the nail with a dot of icing. After the flowers are completed, slip the wax paper off. A No. 67 leaf tube filled with slightly thinned down icing is used for the poinsettias. Starting in the middle of your nail, draw a long narrow leaf out relaxing pressure as you come to the end of your nail. This leaf should be slightly curved. This procedure is followed until six leaves are piped on. A small cone with a No. 3 tip filled with bright yellow icing is used to make the center of the poinsettia. This is completed by piping three small bell-like tips in the center of the poinsettia.

TEA ROSE

Using a No. 104 tube, fill a cone with royal icing. Stick 1½ inch square of waxed paper on your nail with a dot of icing. To start the tea rose, place the cone directly over the nail and squeeze a dot of icing on the nail. Hold the heavy end of the tube to the nail with the narrow end up. With the tube in the center, start squeezing and turning the nail, steps 1 and 2. Continue turning the nail until you have completed two turns around the center as shown in step 3. After completing the bottom portion of the flower dome, go around the top portion in the same manner. The flower dome should stand approximately 1 inch high as shown in step 4. Then place three petals around the top. Starting half way down the dome with the large end of tube touching the dome, squeeze the tube gently and lift. While squeezing turn the nail in your left hand counter clockwise. The first three petals should cling to the dome as shown in step 5. For the four outside petals, start at the very bottom with the large end of tube touching dome and the narrow end out. Move up about ¼ inch from the top and come down on the other side rolling the tube as you go around. This gives the petals a roll back effect as shown in steps 6, 7, and 8.

LILY OF THE VALLEY

In making the Lily of the Valley use a royal icing that may be lifted up and worked into flower arrangements after drying. The two long leaves are made on waxed paper with a No. 67 leaf tube. The cone is filled with thinned down delicate green royal icing. The small white lilies may be worked directly on one of the leaves. A more lifelike effect is obtained by using a thin green cloth-covered wire cut to the proper length and and placed into the leaves as illustrated above. The lilies are then placed on the wire with a small cone of royal icing. These are made by a series of circular motions which simulate a tiny bell.

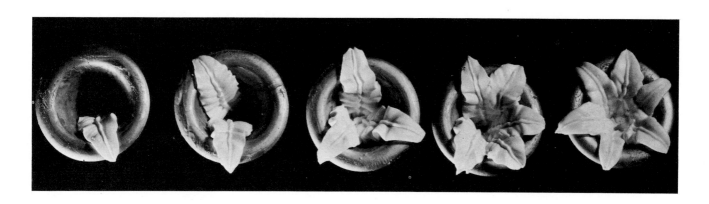

EASTER LILY

A one-ounce glass may be used for making this flower. Grease the glass heavily with lard or shortening to prevent sticking. One glass must be used for each flower. The Easter Lily takes about 24 hours to dry. Use a No. 67 leaf tube and fill the cone full with white royal icing that has been thinned down slightly. Hold the glass in the left hand and make a long leaf starting at the bottom of the glass as shown in step 1. A heavy pressure is used at the base of the leaf, relaxing pressure as you move out toward the tip. Follow steps 2 and 3 making two or more leaves dividing the nail into three sections. The next three leaves are placed between the first. When starting the last three leaves, begin half way up the glass. If you have trouble getting the leaves to come off to a point, the icing isn't quite thin enough or you are not relaxing pressure gradually as you complete the leaf. Four or five yellow stamens are then piped into the center of the flower. When removing the flowers from the glass, heat the glass slightly to melt the grease.

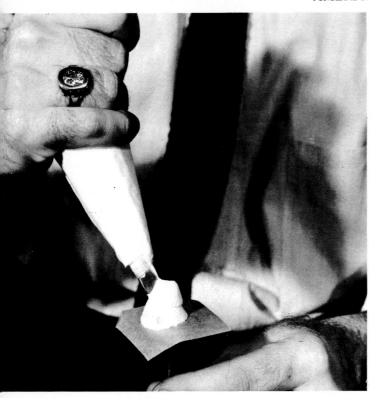

To construct the base of the rose, the cone is held in the right hand with the small end of the tube pointing up and toward the center of the nail. Continue squeezing the cone and turning the nail until you have a fairly wide base. Another dome is then started directly on top of the first dome.

This is the proper position and angle of the tube when making the three small petals around the top portion of the dome which completes the bud.

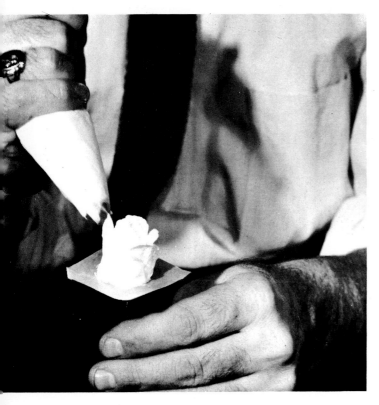

This is the position of the tube when making the second five petals directly under the bud. The petals stand out slightly. To do this the tube must stand out slightly as illustrated.

The last row of petals must stand out. This is accomplished by simply turning the tube out more to the side.

AMERICAN BEAUTY ROSE

As the name implies this is truly an American Beauty and when properly made the rose is the loveliest flower made with the tube. Make this flower with a No. 124 rose tube that has a straight edge and permits control of the "roll" at the petal's edge. Buttercream, royal or boiled icing may be used. Be sure it is stiff enough so that the petals stand up. Strip the cone by using a spatula-knife and pink icing. Start the strips at the base of the tube at the wide opening. Continue it up through the cone. Fill the remainder of the cone with white icing. This gives you a natural two-tone rose effect. Stick a small piece of waxed paper on the head of nail. After the flower is completed slide the paper off the nail onto a pan. With this method as many flowers as desired may be made using one nail.

The first step is to construct the base with a small dome of icing about 1½ inches high. The nail should be turned in a counter clockwise motion. The cone is held in the right hand with the small end of the tube pointing up and slightly toward the center of the nail. Start squeezing the cone and turning the nail. Continue squeezing and turning until you have a fairly wide base. Another dome is then started directly on top of the first dome. Three small petals are then placed around the top part of the dome which completes the bud or top portion of the rose. The next five petals are placed on slightly under the bud and stand out a little more than the petals of the bud. In placing these petals make sure to overlap each one slightly. To complete the last row start at the very bottom of the base. Squeezing while you turn the nail in a co-ordinated motion, lift the tube slightly and then return to the bottom of the base. Continue the petals all the way around the bottom of the dome completing the flower. Here are some common mistakes in making the American Beauty Rose. First: Making the rose too flat. This results when the dome or base of the petals is not high enough or when each row of petals is not started below the preceding row. Second: The petals are too tight. This is caused by holding the tube in toward the dome. Third: Petals are flat looking, caused by holding the tube to the side or away from the dome or base. Fourth: Wavy petals. Squeezing the bag too heavily or turning the nail too slowly will result in this. It is evident why the rose is a difficult flower to execute properly. Have patience and practice it diligently.

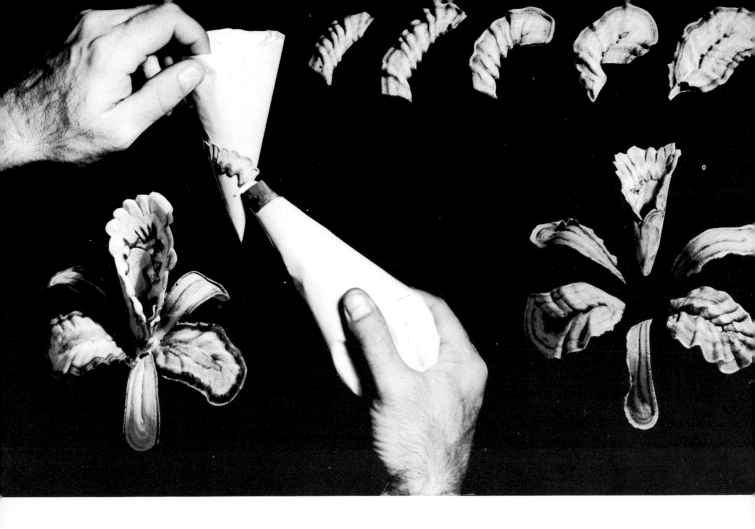

ORCHID

The Orchid is by far the most beautiful and delicate of all the flowers. Seldom will you see an orchid made with a tube. We have always made them in pulled sugar or gumpaste and believe this is the first time this has been illustrated using only a No. 124 tube. Because the orchid is made in six sections and then put together, it must be made of royal icing. Strip one side of a large cone with purple paste color using the brush method described in *Color Technique*. Fill the remainder of the cone with a delicate purple icing. Using a No. 124 tube follow the procedure in step 2 to make the large outside petals. These are made on waxed paper with the large side of the tube touching the paper. The tube is moved up on one side about two inches and then brought down on the other side while maintaining a back and forth motion to create an uneven edge on the outside of the petal Two of these petals must be made for each orchid After making a total of 20 of them in a row, lay the waxed paper over a long roll of about an inch in diameter to give the petals a curved effect. The long narrow petals are made in the same manner. There are three to each orchid and 30 should be made on a sheet. In making these petals, an even steady pressure must be maintained while moving the tube along. These are placed over a long roll in the same manner as the first petals. The most difficult part of

the orchid is making the center which has a sort of inverted cone shape, shown in step 1. This is the main section of the orchid. To make the center, a waxed paper cone approximately four inches high and two inches at the base should be constructed. It is held in a down position and the first part of the center petal is started from the rear of the cone about half way up. After the first half of the petal is completed, turn the cone around and start the second half. As the tube is moved down to the bottom of the cone, a slight back and forth motion must be maintained to create an uneven effect. After working around the cone, the opening in the back must be filled in by simply squeezing and moving the tube over it. The rough area can be smoothed out by dipping the fore-finger in water and running it over the back of the rough area. To store for drying, place the cone over a small bottle such as a pop bottle. This allows the air to dry and harden the petal in about 24 hours. Make ten center petals in this manner.

To assemble the orchid, a small amount of royal icing is piped on waxed paper or directly on the cake. The center of the orchid (the part made around the cone) is placed into the mound standing upright. The two larger petals are placed slightly to the front. Then the three narrower petals are put in place finishing the flower.

LEAVES

Making a leaf properly is as important as making most of your flowers. The essential part of making a leaf is to have the icing at the proper consistency. It must be thinned down so it may be drawn out to a point. All the leaves illustrated on this page were made with a No. 67 tube.

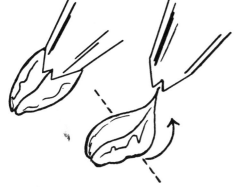

The very tiny leaves in the first row are made by touching the pan, for practice, applying a small amount of pressure. At half way mark move the tube along discontinuing pressure and lifting away from the pan. This will draw a tiny leaf out to a point, as illustrated.

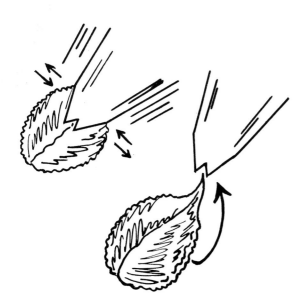

The second row of leaves are slightly larger and have a ruffled edge effect. This is obtained by touching the leaf tube to your pan at a 45 degree angle. Apply pressure and as you squeeze move the tube back and forth in a steady even motion diminishing pressure as you come to the tip of your leaf. Discontinue pressure and continue moving out, thus pulling the leaf off to a point.

The third row of leaves are made in the same manner and with the same tube except they are slightly larger and are to be used on a flower such as the dahlia. For this larger leaf the same procedure was followed except a more pronounced back and forth motion is used as you apply pressure. As you continue to apply pressure this leaf is built up and as you move along coming to the point the pressure is diminished. Finally relax pressure altogether and move away, thus breaking the leaf off to a point.

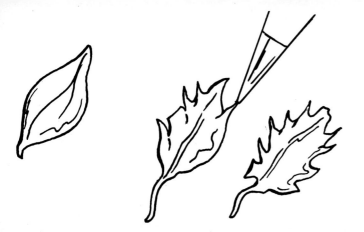

The first three leaves are a simulated holly leaf. This is made by first making a regular leaf with your No. 67 leaf tube. To obtain the pointed effect on the edges of the leaves, a small cone with a No. 3 tube is filled with thinned down icing. The cone is placed into the side of the leaf. A small amount of pressure is applied to the cone and as you move away discontinue pressure, thus forming the points on the leaf. The three other leaf variations in this row were formed by simply working three or more leaves into a pattern as illustrated.

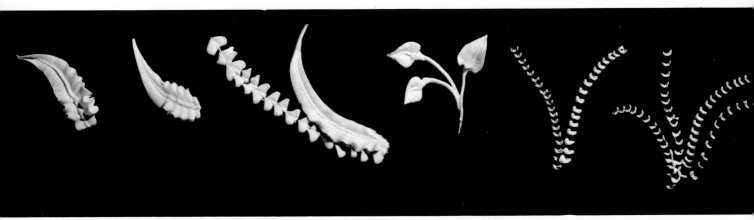

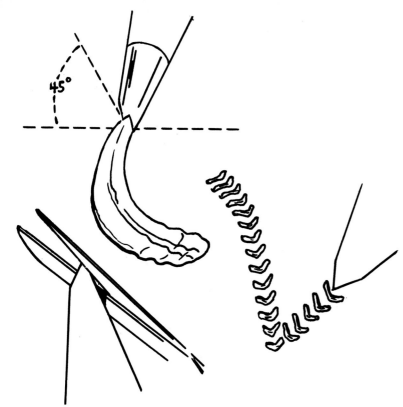

CUTTING FERN TIP

The above illustrates a few variations of leaves. The first leaf is the leaf we use for lily of the valley, yellow jonquil, or any other long narrow leaf. To make a leaf such as this, a No. 67 leaf tube was used. As you apply pressure the tube is tipped slightly to one side. By moving off at an angle the tube tipped to the side—the pressure is first built up and then diminished as you move the tube along. Finally discontinuing pressure altogether continue moving, thus breaking the leaf off to a point.

The third step illustrates small tiny leaves being worked off a long leaf. These tiny leaves are formed by simply squeezing and touching the pan, for practice.

The fourth step in the last row shows three small leaves worked into a stem. The leaves are first piped on as explained above and the stems are worked into the leaves with the use of a No. 3 tube.

The fern in the right hand corner was made by cutting the cone in the following manner. Make a small paper cone with a very small point. Fill the cone up with green icing and force the icing down to the base of the cone. Squeeze the cone together and cut the tip off to a point. See illustration under cutting Fern tip. We suggest you practice an entire pan of leaves before placing them on your cake tops.

CHAPTER IV

Figure Piping

Figure piping is an interesting subject normally looked upon as being advanced and difficult work. Two reasons the novice encounters so much difficulty in figure piping are: Improper consistency of the icings. Following incorrect procedures. In training over 4000 cake decorators, we have developed a new and simple way of figure piping. By following the simple steps, you can do a good job in a short time.

There are two distinct methods of figure piping. The *fill-in method* and the *pressure formation method*. The fill-in method is accomplished by drawing an outline of the subject and then filling in with icing. The pressure formation method is a technique of pressure control. By squeezing and relaxing pressure as the cone is moved along, almost any formation in icings can be obtained.

For best results, boiled icing, royal icing, or piping jelly is used. In using icings it is imperative that the icings be whipped thoroughly and then thinned down slightly. When it is squeezed through the cone, it flows out smoothly and does not roll. If it is too thin, the icing will not hold its shape. After the proper steps are known, your only mistake will be in your pressure control.

We will start with the very simple type of figure piping and gradually work up to the more intricate figures.

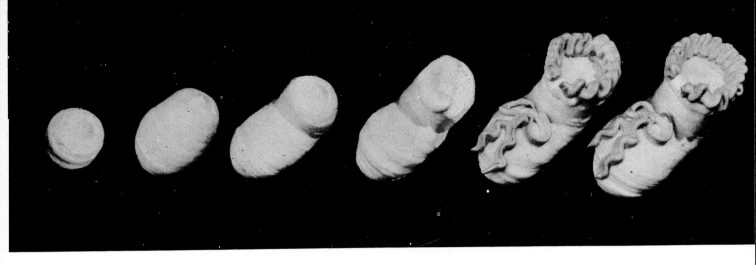

BABY BOOTIES

Either boiled or royal icing must be used for the figure piping of the bootie. If you desire, the bootie may be piped in royal icing on waxed paper and used at a later date. Insert a No. 4 tube in a cone filled with icing. Holding the cone straight up, apply pressure keeping the tube ⅛" off the surface. As the icing builds up, *step 1,* continue to lift the cone until it is about ½" off the pan. Keep applying pressure and move back as you squeeze until a mound of icing approximately 1½" long and ½" high is formed as illustrated. Circular movements are used to form the open portion or the top of the bootie.

The bootie is then trimmed using a No. 3 tube in a contrasting color. To obtain the ruffled effect, the tube is moved in a series of up and down motions while squeezing. The tying of the bow is done by a small figure 8 with two streamers.

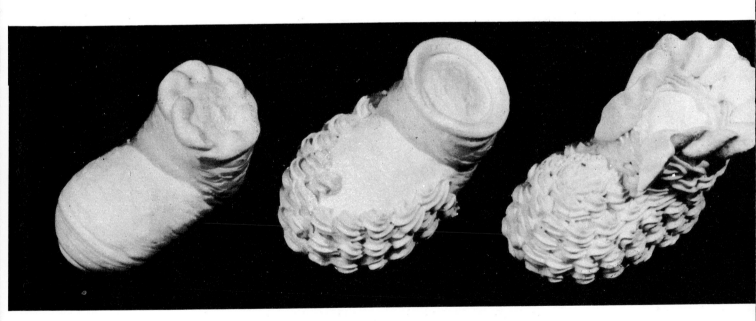

LARGE KNITTED BABY BOOTIE

To complete this large bootie, a slightly stiffer icing must be used in order to hold its shape. After filling a large cone, cut the tip off to a 3/16" opening. The same procedure is followed as in the construction of the smaller bootie except that as the pressure is applied, lift the cone up to a height of about 1¼". The higher the cone is lifted, the higher the baby bootie will be. After the bootie is formed, the entire outside is given a knitted effect. This is accomplished with a small star tube stripped in pink icing. Moving the tube back and forth will give the bootie a knitted effect as illustrated. The bootie is then trimmed with a ribbon using a No. 104 tube. Starting at the upper back edge, ruffle the tube as the pressure is applied. Repeat the operation on the other side. If the bootie is made in royal icing, pipe on waxed paper and place on the cake after drying.

STORK

Two cones are used for the piping of a stork. Fill a small cone with white icing using a No. 4 tube. Fill another small cone with pastel pink icing using a No. 3 tube. In figure piping the head use the No. 4 tube. After a round dot is formed two long lines are piped in with a No. 3 tube, completing the bill. The neck is made in the same manner as in the swan although not so curved.

The body is tear-drop shaped and slanted down at a 45 degree angle. The feathers are worked into the body with a No. 4 tube as illustrated. The legs are made with the pastel pink icing and the No. 3 tube. To make the upper parts of the legs thicker, apply pressure and move the cone very slowly. As the line builds up, relax pressure slightly and continue moving down. At the knuckle joint of the stork, apply slightly more pressure. As the joint builds, relax pressure again and continue moving down until the end of the leg is reached. The claws are a series of three or four small movements. The diaper is placed under the storks bill by squeezing strongly at the base and relaxing pressure as you move up forming the diaper. The small baby in pink may be piped into the diaper, if desired. For a cake top, the stork may be completed by working a few green leaves and stems around and using a small cone of brown icing to pipe in the cattails.

BIRD IN FLIGHT

With a No. 3 tube, make a small cone. Strip the cone in pink or blue using the brush method. Fill the cone with a slightly thinned down icing or piping jelly. Hold the cone just off the surface and make a curved line for the outer edge of the wing as illustrated. The next line is made smaller still following the same curve as the first line until the wing is completed. The tail is piped next in much the same way as the wing, however, the lines are straight as illustrated. The body is made by holding the tube at a 45 degree angle starting about half way back from the tail. As pres-

sure is increased, move the cone forward and continue adding pressure until the breast is built up.

The head is formed by easing off on pressure and drawing out a small string of icing. The string is then brought around in a circular motion and by touching the string to the head and squeezing slightly the bill is formed. The inner wing is put on next. Start from the inside making a small curve, and then continue moving out with back and forward strokes until the completed wing is obtained.

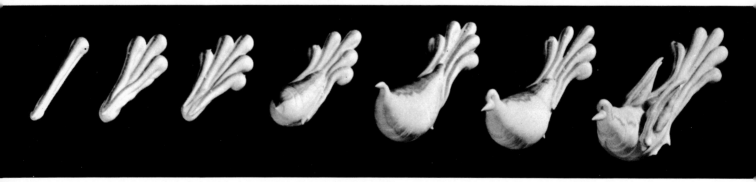

DOVE

Insert a No. 3 tube into a small cone and fill with slightly thinned down icing. To make the tail, hold the tube slightly above and perpendicular to the surface. With a series of back and forth motions and a slight amount of pressure, the lines are formed for the tail as illustrated. To make the body, stick the tube into the icing and hold it at a 45 degree angle. Apply pressure and move forward slightly. When the body

builds up, relax pressure and continue moving up until the body is formed as illustrated. Bring the string around in a circular motion to form the head. Touch the string against the body, pull out and relax pressure forming the bill. Using the same tube, the two wings are formed by sticking the tube into the body, squeezing heavily and moving away. This will form a base that is over-piped to form the wing.

PIPING A SWAN

Place a No. 3 tube in a small cone filled with icing or piping jelly.

Step No. 1 is the piping of the head. Holding the cone tip 1/16" off the surface, make a round dot by applying pressure and stopping. After making the dot, ease off the pressure as you move out to the tip of the bill. This will break the bill off to a point as illustrated.

Step No. 2 is the neck – With one smooth motion starting with the tube inside the head, come down to form a smooth question mark. The tube is still held off the surface.

Step No. 3 is the body – Begin at the lower curve of the neck holding the tube about ¼" off the surface in a stationary position and squeeze. The icing will flow out evenly forming a circle. As it begins to build up, lift the tube ¼" higher as you squeeze and then start easing off on pressure slowly and bring the tube back to the surface or the cake top. Stop squeezing at the end of the tail and continue moving the tube out to bring the tail to a point.

Step No. 4 is the wing – Place the tube in the body and squeeze while moving at a 45 degree angle away from the body easing off the pressure as you go. With a little practice, this figure will be easy to form. Once made properly, any size can be piped simply by using a larger or smaller tip and applying pressure proportionately.

THE TROPICAL BIRD

The Tropical Bird is completed in much the same manner as the Bird in Flight. Using a No. 3 tube, strip the tube with the brush method in two bright paste colors. Fill the cone with a slightly thinned down boiled icing or piping jelly. After the wing is formed, the tail is brought down to an angle giving the body an elongated look. The body is formed in the same manner as the Bird in Flight. After completing the head, the tuft of feathers on the head is obtained by squeezing and pulling away slightly from the head. Use a combination of bright colors for your stripping. A beautiful effect in colors gives this bird an unusual tropical appearance.

THE WITCH

Place a No. 4 tube in a small cone and fill with a slightly thinned down icing. Holding the cone perpendicular to the pan (for practice) and about 1/16″ off the pan, make the nose by squeezing strongly, then lightly, moving the tube in a hook motion as illustrated in Step 1. The chin is made in the same manner, starting at the base of the nose and moving down. Ease off on pressure and return in a circular motion to the starting point forming the chin. For the forehead, start above the nose and with one movement come down to meet the chin. Next, the hair is filled in. The hat is then piped on and the brim is piped over the hair as illustrated.

Once the head is completed the body is simple. In piping it, a much greater pressure must be used and the tube must be held ¼″ to ½″ away from the pan. Starting from the chin, move down at an angle, squeezing very strongly, completing the trunk, continue out to complete the leg. The second leg is then piped on. The next step is to pipe the inside arm. After this is completed the broom is piped in. The outside arm is piped on next. The dress is filled in last.

After a little practice, you should be able to pipe the witch on a cake top in approximately two minutes. The worse looking the witch's face is, the more realistic she becomes.

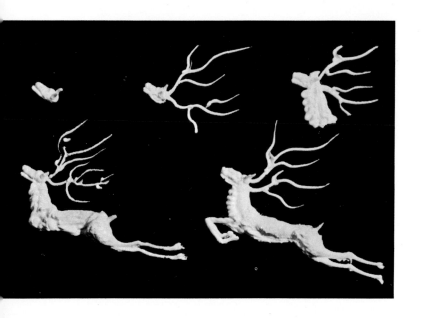

REINDEER

Place a No. 3 tube in a small cone and fill with white icing. The upper portion of the mouth and head are piped first, then the lower jaw. The antlers and neck are piped on. Move down in an arch and complete the body.

The rear right leg is piped on, then the left leg and last the two front legs are piped on.

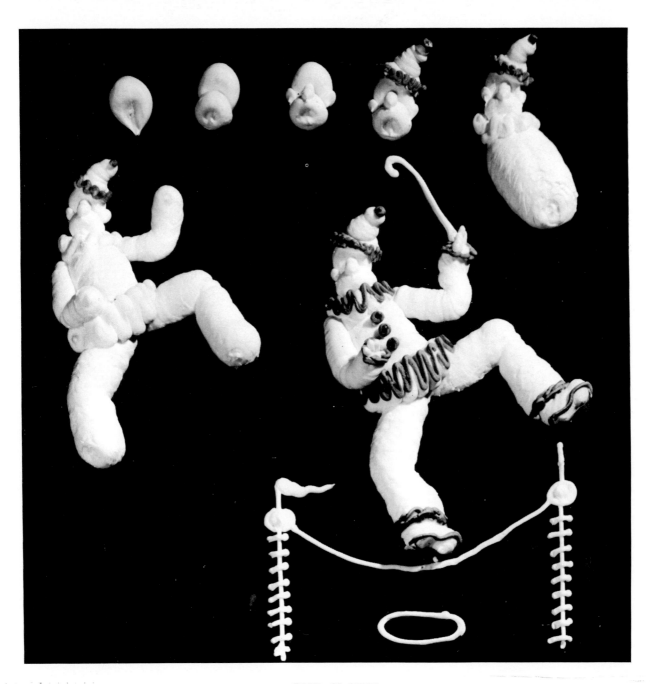

THE CLOWN

Floral and border designs might not appeal especially to children, but the clown is ideal for attracting and holding their attention. Insert a No 4 tube into a large cone and fill with icing. To figure pipe the clown, we will begin by making the head. Make a large round dot by squeezing and gradually lifting ½″ off the surface. After forming the dot, ease off pressure and cut through the dot back down to the surface as illustrated. Another dot is then made directly below the first, continue to squeeze until the second dot overlaps the lower portion of the first dot. The nose is made by placing the tube inside the head and squeezing slightly. The ears are made and placed on by appropriately shaped dots of icing. The hat is started at the crown of the head. Using heavy pressure, move upward and relax pressure. The ruffled brim of the hat is merely a weaving string of icing in a contrasting color. The body is piped by squeezing heavily and holding the tube ½″ off the surface. As the icing builds up, move slowly down as illustrated. The legs are formed starting at the waist by using a heavy pressure and moving in the direction illustrated. The arms are formed in the same manner starting inside the body. After piping in the feet, the suit is trimmed with ruffles at the neck and waist in a contrasting color.

The clown may be made in many different positions. Another method of making this clown is to pipe it in royal icing on waxed paper. After it is completely piped out, bend the waxed paper at the waist in a sitting position. When the royal icing drys the waxed paper may be peeled off and the clown will be in a sitting position and may be placed on the cake.

THE PEACOCK

Using the No. 3, the No. 4 and the No. 16 tubes, fill three small cones with icing. Starting at the tail, draw a small fan-shaped oblong, as illustrated, with a No. 16 tube. The fan is then filled in with icing starting very small at the tip of the tail and building up as you come toward the body.

The eyes or half circles to simulate the feathers are piped in using the No. 16 tube. The body is then built up with a No. 4 tube. Stick the tube directly into the tail and squeeze very strongly. As the body builds up, move the tube up and relax the pressure slightly form-

ing the upper part of the neck. As you come up to the head, relax pressure and get a string from the icing. Stop squeezing and bring the string around in a circular motion and touch. Bring the string out, discontinue pressure and pull away forming the bill. The wings are then worked into the body with a No. 16 tube and overpiped with a No. 4 tube. The tiny feathers around the base of the tail are worked in with a No. 3 tube. After the bird is complete the vivid coloring effect may be obtained by spraying with an atomizer.

THE FILL-IN METHOD OF FIGURE PIPING

The Wiltons have devised this method of figure piping making it possible for the beginner to pipe almost any type of figure he desires. Here are a few of the numerous figures that can be piped out simply by following a pattern as we have illustrated. The patterns used should be side views and not over 2 to 4 inches high. A large pattern would be difficult to fill in. For the fill-in method you must use royal icing.

BALLET DANCERS

To figure pipe the ballet dancers, three small cones were used. A No. 4 tube with pink icing, a No. 3 tube with pink icing and a No. 4 tube with purple icing. To perform the *fill in* method properly, first obtain a small picture of a ballerina figure as illustrated. Using a thin piece of parchment paper trace the ballerina figure on the paper. Cut out a small piece of waxed paper and lay it over the traced ballerina figure. Using the original figure as a guide begin to fill in on your traced ballerina. The face is made first with a No. 3 tube. The hair is then filled in, followed by the ballerina skirt with the No. 4 tube in purple. The arms and legs are in pink. When coming to a small portion such as the hand, use the No. 3 tube.

ROCKET SHIP AND SPACE MAN

The Rocket Ship is made following the same Fill-in procedure as for the Ballet Dancer but is easier to make because it has no fine features. It is made in a deep red and blue by using two small cones and a No. 4 tube — one cone filled with red and one with blue Royal Icing. Start at the base, or heavy end of the Rocket Ship and move your cone slowly towards the point applying heavy pressure to obtain the de-

sired diameter. As you come to the point of the Rocket Ship relax pressure until the tip is completed.

The Space Man is made following the same fill-in procedure as used for the Ballet Dancer. The head is filled in with a No. 3 tube using pink Royal Icing. The hair is made with a No. 3 tube using yellow icing. The space suit is made with a No. 4 tube using a deep blue icing. The suit is trimmed in yellow using a No. 3 tube.

LAMBS

Use a No. 4 tube to pipe the lambs, start filling in at the head and working down to the body, the hind legs and the front legs.

A piece of waxed paper is placed over your outline and you pipe directly on top of the waxed paper following the outline that shows through. When the icing hardens, the waxed paper is peeled off the figure.

RABBIT AND WAGON

The rabbit was piped in brilliant colors using the No. 4 tube. The wagon was piped in a contrasting color with many vivid colors in the flowers.

DOG

The dog was piped in brown icing with a No. 4 tube.

CAMEL

To pipe the camel, a No. 4 tube is used. Starting at the head, work down to the neck and then around the two humps to the back. The back right leg is piped first and then the left leg. The front right leg is then piped and then the left leg.

GIRAFFE

For the giraffe a No. 4 tube is also used, starting at the head, work up to the neck and come around to the left hind leg. The two front legs are piped next and then the right hind leg is piped on.

MONKEY

For the monkey, we use a No. 4 tube, starting with the head, then the body, followed by the legs and last the arms. The monkey was put into deep green foliage with tiny yellow flowers worked around for the color effect.

CHAPTER V

Tube Writing and Lettering

To write properly with an icing it is most important to use a thinned down icing or a piping jelly. By using a thin icing it is possible to draw out thin lines without having the lines break. Before attempting writing, you must realize that it is possible to write very beautifully on a cake and still have a very bad script with a pen. In writing with a pen we normally use the fingers for our various curves and lines. Using the tube, we move the entire arm.

Every decorator, after he becomes fairly efficient in tube writing, will have a recognized style of his own. Before attempting to write on a cake you will find it much easier to practice on a hard surface, such as a cookie pan.

Take a small cone and fill it with a thinned down white icing. If you care to, you may use a small brush. Dip it into a bright paste color and run a small line of paste color down the inside of the cone. Then add the icing. This will give you an unusual two-tone effect and will help your writing look more attractive. The icing is squeezed down to the bottom of the cone and a very tiny opening is cut. If you care to, you may use a No. 3 tube for the tip instead of cutting your cone. The tube is held with the thumb and the first two fingers. The first practice steps should be a series of long easy back and forth motions as illustrated. For these practice movements and practice writing, we suggest that you begin by resting your cone on the pan at an angle. Then move it back and forth very lightly always touching the pan to help you to obtain a smooth even line. Later on when you become efficient in your writing and various curves and swings, you may lift the tube up very slightly. In order to do fine writing on a cake top, it is necessary to glide your tube over the icing very lightly without digging in. If you lift your cone completely off the cake top, it is impossible to do the fine type of writing. After you become efficient in making these lines by resting the cone on the cake lift it slightly and glide it very gently over the top of the pan. This is the technique that is necessary when working directly on a cake top.

After becoming efficient with the back and forth motion on the down stroke, make a slight pause as you come down to obtain the built up effect as illustrated.

Going up use a steady pressure. On the down stroke use a slight back and forth motion. This will give you the attractive built up effect. The next thing to practice is a series of small "c's." Move the tube down in a graceful easy curved swing without stopping. After practicing one or two pans of this type of curve, the next type is a continuous capital "E". This type of tube writing will help you obtain neatness and uniformity. After practicing these various curves, circles and lines, the next step is the "Happy Birthday", the most common example of tube writing. We suggest that the inscription be put on the cake first and followed by the floral spray. In writing the "Happy Birthday" you must realize you have a very limited space and often too much writing must be crowded into the small space. By keeping your letters in the "Happy" long and very narrow with only a small amount of space between each letter, your writing will look fancy and will not take as much room on a cake top. In the writing of "Happy", the first line of the "H" is made. The second line of the "H" is brought down very close to the first and is crossed. The "A" is started as close to the "H" as possible and made long and narrow. We come straight up to the "P" and straight down. Then we pick it up and finish off the "P." For the next one, straight up line and straight down, then we pick the

"P" up and finish it off at the top. The "Y" is made and as you come down start an easy, graceful flowing line to finish the "Happy."

The "Birthday" you will find is a little more difficult because of the number of letters that must be made. If you bear in mind that these letters must be long and narrow and when finishing off a letter to use a nice gracefully curved line, you will help give it the fancy effect.

If you care to, you may first write very simply. Then after the inscription is placed on the cake, you may go over it to achieve the built up effect. We suggest that this build up should be done as you write each letter. On the "Happy Birthday" in the "H" as you come down on the straight line for the "H", a slight back and forth motion is maintained to create that build up. In working the "A" on the down stroke of the "A," a back and forth motion is maintained and the same with the two "p's" coming on the long down stroke using the back and forth motion. This is a time saving method. After becoming proficient in writing "Happy Birthday," you may then go on to "Mother" and then "Congratulations," "Sweet Sixteen," etc.

We suggest that you spend five minutes a day for four or five days on each inscription.

LETTERING

In an effort to familiarize the student with what may be considered good lettering design for cake decorating purposes, we have devoted the next few pages to three representative styles with complete alphabets. The letters are large enough to be traced directly or they may be used as guides to prepare alphabets in other sizes.

Individual letters in a word may be evenly spaced, but the lettering will be more pleasing to the eye if the spacing is adjusted according to the open space in and around each letter. For example: O's and C's have large open spaces and may be placed more closely to adjacent letters, while I's, M's, N's, etc., should have more space.

As far as technique is concerned, we feel that almost any style of lettering can be mastered by the student with moderate practice.

The student might begin with the following method: Lay a piece of waxed paper over any of the examples of lettering illustrated on these pages. Then using a cone with the proper sized tube, the letters beneath the waxed paper may be used as guides. Some styles such as the Old English will require two tube sizes for the thick and thin lines, while the Free Script and Modern Block styles may be rendered with a single tube size. After you are satisfied with your proficiency, the wax paper may be abandoned and you are ready to work directly on the cake.

Merry Christmas

Sweet Sixteen

Happy New Year

A B C D E F G
H I J K L M N
O P Q R S T U
V W X Y Z a b c d
e f g h i j k l m n o p q
r s t u v w x y z

1 2 3 4 5 6 7 8 9 0

Mother

OLD ENGLISH

This beautiful style dates back to early medieval times when it was employed in many variations in religious writings. This lettering style will probably require more practice than any other because of the variation in stroke thickness, but the handsome effect is well worth the effort.

To My Valentine

Happy Birthday

A B C D E F G H I J

K L M N O P Q R

S T U V W X Y Z

abcdefghijklmnopqrstuvwxyz

1234567890 &

FREE SCRIPT

There may be as many variations of this continuous script style as there are individuals using it. In fact, after the student acquires some measure of skill, his own handwriting will have a noticeable influence on the results.

Bon Voyage

Congratulations

ABCDEFGHIJK
LMNOPQRST
UVWXYZabc
defghijklmno
pqrstuvwxyz
1234567890

MODERN BLOCK

This bold, easy to read lettering style will be easy to master and lends itself admirably to almost any requirement. Careful attention to spacing is necessary for best results.

CHAPTER VI

Gum Paste

Gumpaste is nothing more than cornstarch, powdered sugar, gelatin and water. When this mixture is worked together properly it has a consistency of pie dough and may be handled in much the same way as clay. It can be rolled out on a table in thin sheets and cut into various forms and patterns and left to dry. After drying they may be placed together with royal icing to form any particular desired pattern. Gumpaste may also be molded into various designs and shapes by using plates, glass ware or silver trays for the pattern. Using patterns and molds, with very little freehand work, gumpaste work becomes child's play. Many of your own original ideas may be created in gumpaste. By adding a few drops of peppermint to your gumpaste, the gumpaste will taste much like a mint lozenge when dried completely.

Recipe:

¼ oz. gelatin (one envelope equals ¼ oz.)
½ cup water
1 level teaspoon cream of tartar
Place on low heat and stir. When dissolved add:
4 cups powdered sugar

1 cup cornstarch
Work like a pie dough.
After mixing well in a bowl, cover with a damp cloth. Gumpaste handles much like pie dough. Cornstarch is used for dusting the table to prevent sticking.

To make some of the objects as illustrated here, the table is first dusted with cornstarch. A small piece of gumpaste is placed on the table, padded out slightly by hand and dusted with cornstarch on the top. Then roll with a rolling pin to about ⅛ inch thickness. The mold that you use is then dusted with cornstarch. The rolled out gumpaste is forced into the desired mold. A sharp instrument is used to cut around the mold, and the gumpaste is allowed to dry in the mold for approximately 12 hours.

GUMPASTE DESSERT CUP

To make these gumpaste dessert cups, begin by dusting your table with cornstarch. Roll a sheet of gumpaste to ⅛″ in thickness. The gumpaste is then cut into circles approximately 3″ in diameter. The circles are put into cupcake tins dusted with cornstarch. After the gumpaste dries, a No. 104 tube filled with a pastel pink royal icing is used to put the ruffle around the top portion of the gumpaste tray as illustrated. After the dessert is placed into the cup, an American beauty rose (which was piped out in advance) can be placed on top of the ice cream as illustrated.

GUMPASTE SWAN

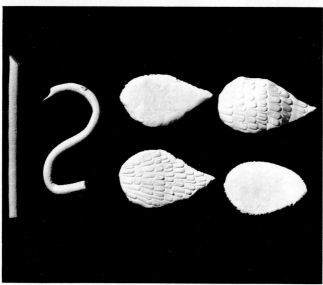

There are four sections to the swan: the neck, the two wings and the base. To construct the neck, roll out a piece of gumpaste approximately ⅜″ in diameter. Cut off at an angle as shown in the illustration. The bill and head are then formed by *squeezing the angle down to a flat point.* The two wings are then cut from gumpaste to simulate a large leaf. A paper clip was used to create the feathered effect. To obtain the cup or rounded shape of the wing, two small mounds of cornstarch are placed on a flat surface and the wing is formed over this mound. The base is cut out like the wing and turned up slightly at the tail. After 24 hours of drying the four sections are then stuck together with royal icing. The neck is fastened to the base first, then the two wings to the neck.

All of the Gum Paste Work shown on this page can be done quickly.

Roll out a layer of Gum Paste to approximately ⅛ inch thickness. Dust the tray, compote or gravy boat with cornstarch to prevent the Gum Paste from sticking to it. Place the Gum Paste in the form being molded so that it conforms with the object being shaped. Cut off the excess Gum Paste with a sharp knife. Let dry for 12 to 24 hours.

Base and handles are made of Gum Paste. When dry they can be stuck to the main form with Royal Icing.

The upright string work is done by turning the Gum Paste compote upside down and by doing the string work in thinned-down Royal Icing. After the icing dries, turn the compote right side up and the fence like effect is obtained.

By following a pattern, or using a mold, any object may be made of Gum Paste without difficulty and with very little practice.

After the Gum Paste Molds have dried they can be further decorated with fancy flowers and borders.

CHAPTER VII

Candy and Sugar Mold

"Character-Candy" Mold is a delicious taste treat for children and adults alike. It is easily made from the Wilton Prepared Candy Mold Mix and can be purchased in six popular flavors, Cherry, Grape, Root-Beer, Orange, Lemon and Lime each vividly colored. Candy is so simple to prepare and such fun, it will be difficult for mother to stop everyone from getting into the act.

"Character Candy" Mold is easily made by following this recipe: Add 3 teaspoons of warm water to a packet of Wilton Candy Mold Prepared Mix and mix with 2 cups of granulated sugar. Follow the steps illustrated below.

Sugar Mold, used almost exclusively for the decoration of cakes is made by mixing 3 teaspoons of warm water to 3 teaspoons of Wilton Deluxe Meringue then adding Wilton Paste Coloring to achieve the color desired. (Remember these colors are highly concentrated and a little goes a long way). Form a paste of these ingredients and add 2 cups of granulated sugar. To mix see illustrations below.

Blend Wilton Candy Mix and sugar together using a large spoon, or the best way to mix them thoroughly is to rub the sugar and paste between the palms of the hands and through the fingers until it is worked evenly throughout the granulated sugar.

In humid climates the mold should be dusted before mixture is inserted. To accomplish this place 4 tablespoons of cornstarch in a thin cloth and tie to form a bag. Dust mold lightly with this bag.

Pack mixture solidly into mold and scrape off excess with a knife.

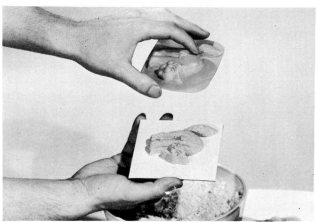

Place pre-cut cardboard square over mold and turn gently upside down as illustrated. Candy may be swiftly dried, by placing candy in preheated oven (200°) for 5 minutes or placing in direct sunlight.

There is never any waste with Wilton Candy Mix — this delightful confection may be kept indefinitely without refrigeration. Unused mixture can also be kept by placing it in sealed container and storing in the refrigerator for future use.

3 complete sets of Wilton "Character-Candy" molds are available. Each set is designed to delight both adults and children. The Mother Goose Set is preferred by smaller tots as a special treat at their parties. This set consists of 8 individual "Character-Candy" plastic molds in the form of favorite nursery rhyme characters: Mary, Mary, Quite Contrary, The Three Little Pigs, Little Bo-Peep, Little Boy Blue, The Cow Who Jumped Over the Moon, Jack and Jill, and Mother Goose. The Wilton "Character-Candy" Zoo Mold includes 8 plastic forms consisting of a monkey, giraffe, tiger, bear, lion, elephant, horse, and rabbit. These animals are wonderful for decorating birthday cakes and for children's candy sales. Mothers will find them wonderful for fund raising sales of their own. Wilton also produces a "Character-Candy" Holiday set of 8 molds including New Year's and Wedding Bell, Clown and Angel Candle Holders, Valentine's Day Cupid, Halloween Cat, Thanksgiving Cornucopia, Santa Claus, Baby Shower Booties, and a Mother's Day and Easter Flower Basket.

ZOO SET	MOTHER GOOSE SET	HOLIDAY SET
Monkey	"Mary, Mary, Quite Contrary"	Bell
Giraffe	"Little Bo-Peep"	Clown and Angel
Tiger	"The Cow Jumped Over the Moon"	Cupid
Bear	"The Three Little Pigs"	Cat
Lion	"Humpty Dumpty"	Cornucopia
Elephant	"Jack and Jill"	Santa Claus
Horse	"Mother Goose"	Booties
Rabbit	"Little Boy Blue"	Flower Basket

MULTI-COLORING

Different colors and flavors can be used in one mold by mixing separate batches of Wilton Prepared Mix and applying the colors in the mold where desired. Faces and figures can be artfully colored by inserting the desired shades in the mold with a toothpick or other sharp implement, then packing the remainder of the mold with bulk mix. Children love to choose their own color schemes—with Root Beer Monkeys, Lime Tigers and Cherry Elephants becoming the rage.

CHARACTER-CANDY

"Character-Candy" is especially popular among the children for its delicious taste, and the fun and simplicity of its preparation. Kiddies love it for their candy sales, and for their parties. "Character-Candy" can be strung with ribbon and hung gaily around the room as an ornamental party decoration. It's a favorite cake decoration when placed on the top or sides of cakes and a real conversation piece when served in a drink.

CHARACTER-CANDY HUMPTY DUMPTY CAKE

Just right for little tot's birthday parties or as a special treat! To decorate, first frost cake in bright yellow icing. Insert No. 4 Tube in decorating bag to form Humpty Dumpty Brick Wall by holding bag at a 45° angle. Grass trim is done with this same tube and colorful green icing. Humpty Dumpty Character Candy figures are placed on sides and top of cake last.

CHARACTER CANDY EASTER CAKE

Looks so professional, yet is so simple to make! Boiled or marshmallow icing is used to form the fluffy stucco effect frosting. Character Candy Bunny forms are placed on cake top and sides, then colorful jelly beans inserted as shown above.

CHARACTER-CANDY HALLOWEEN CAKE

Can be easily decorated by first icing your cake in gay orange frosting. Then insert No. 30 Star Tube in Decorating bag filled with Chocolate icing (Add cocoa to brown colored icing). Use circular motion to apply top border.

Fence can be piped on with chocolate icing, also. Finish off cake by inserting the pre-made Character-Candy Halloween cats on the sides and top of your cake.

THANKSGIVING—HORN OF PLENTY CHARACTER-CANDY CAKE

Frost cake heavily with colorful yellow icing. Apply bottom button border with No. 30 Star Tube inserted in decorating bag filled with Chocolate Icing. Top Sway border is applied with a No. 4 Tip and Straw-colored icing. Leaves are then made on cake with decorator leaf tube. Drop flowers are added as described in preceding chapter. 2-tone Horn of Plenty is pre-molded by inserting purple and yellow Candy Mix into mold in desired sections.

NEW YEAR CHARACTER CANDY CAKE

Beautifully decorated cake, ideal for New Year's parties. Cake is heavily frosted with white icing. The Bottom Button Border is applied with a No. 30 Star Tube by holding bag at a perpendicular angle and applying gentle pressure while moving in a circular motion. Top border is formed in this same fashion. Pre-Molded Character-Candy Bell is then placed on top of cake and a gaily colored ribbon added for a festive touch.

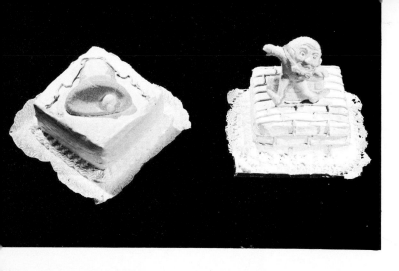

WEDDING or NEW YEAR'S BELL

Ice cake. Make the Sway Border around the base with a No. 30 tube. Place two-color Bell on top. Pipe in ribbon with a No. 4 tube.

HUMPTY DUMPTY

Ice cake. Make the Star Flower Border around the base with a No. 30 tube. Make the brickwork with a No. 4 tube. Place Humpty-Dumpty on top. Brace him at back with a mound of icing.

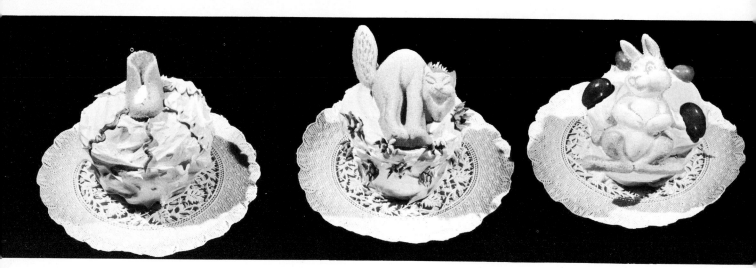

"CHARACTER-CANDY" CUP CAKES

BABY BOOTY

Frost the cup cake. Place "Character-Candy" Baby Booty on top of cake. Use a No. 4 tube to make several curlycue lines coming out from booty.

HALLOWEEN CAT

Frost the cup cake. Place "Character-Candy" Halloween Cat on top. Use a No. 4 tube and make a series of clumps of grass around cat and sides of cake.

EASTER BUNNY

Frost the cup cake. Place "Character-Candy" Easter Bunny on a slant down one side and over top of cup cake. Place colored jelly beans around cake.

Completed baskets and cups made from the candy mold method. The sugar basket in the upper left hand corner was made by placing one mold upside down and the other right side up. These were fastened together with royal icing. The sugar basket may be trimmed in a contrasting color using a small star tube with royal icing. The sugar basket on the upper right hand corner was made from the flat rectangular Jello mold. A handle was made on waxed paper in royal icing. After drying it is set upright with royal icing. These individual cups or baskets may be used to hold candies, nuts, or even ice cream if it is served immediately after the ice cream is placed into the sugar mold.

Cookies and Pastries

Decorating may be used on many kinds of food and is not confined to cakes alone. Once the decorating technique is acquired, it may be used equally well on cupcakes, petits fours, French pastries, Jello, pies and salads. The same procedure is followed throughout; the only things that change are the ingredients of the decorating formula and this occurs only when working on salads or hors d'oeuvres. Instead of using an icing, we use a cream cheese. When worked to the proper consistency, the results are the same.

CUPCAKES
Here are a few ideas for cupcake decorations. A No. 16 tube was used for most of these designs. Any one of our decorating icings may be used for the designs.

This is another way of decorating a cupcake. The top portion of the cake is sliced off and cut in half down the center. The bottom section is iced heavily with buttercream. The two half sections are then placed in an upright position to simulate a basket. The cupcake may be decorated with nuts and cherries.

A clown was iced in white. The ruffle was piped on in a bright color using the No. 104 tube. The arms were piped on with a No. 4 tube. A small ball of freshly beaten icing was piped on for the head with the No. 4 tube. The hat is made by diminishing the pressure as you move up. It is then trimmed in a bright colored icing.

The snowman was made by first icing the cupcake in white. Two mounds were then piped on top to simulate the body and the head. The hat was piped on with a dark icing in a series of circular movements.

The drum was made by cutting off the rounded part of the cupcake. The top and bottom border of the drum were made with a No. 103 tube by simply running the tube along the edge of the cupcake. The drumsticks and the criss-cross design were made with a No. 4 tube.

The basket is made by cutting off the rounded portion of the cupcake. The cupcake is then woven in yellow icing with a No. 16 tube. The handle was made in royal icing ahead of time on waxed paper and allowed to dry.

After filling the basket with tiny rose buds or candies, the handle was then put into place.

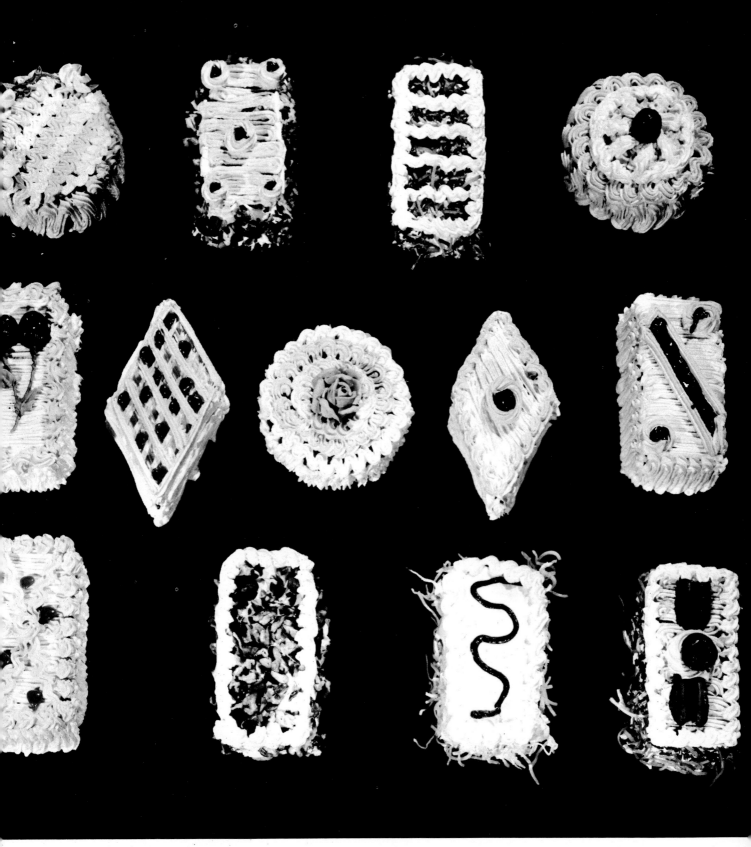

FRENCH PASTRIES

The designs are worked out in pastel colors and in some cases were decorated with a small amount of jelly piped through a No. 3 tube. Some may be rolled or sprinkled with toasted cocoanut or ground almonds.

These French pastries were decorated with a No. 16 star tube using French buttercream (see icing recipes). The circular, oblong and triangular pieces of cake were first sliced in half and iced in a layer of buttercream.

ICING PETITS FOURS

Petits fours are small pieces of cake cut into different designs. These may be iced with a heated fondant or you may use the recipe below.

Petits Fours are placed on a screen and the icing is poured over them as illustrated. The icing that drains off may be saved and re-heated for further pouring.

If you are going to cover only a few pieces, you may do so by spooning the fondant icing over the object.

llustrated here are a few samples of the many attractive ideas that may be carried out when decorating etits fours.

Petits fours may be decorated in a buttercream or boiled icing. The small rosettes are made with a No. 6 tube and red jelly may be piped in the center.

PETITS FOURS ICING

Recipe:
4½ oz. water
6 cups powdered sugar
2 tablespoons corn syrup
A few drops vanilla flavoring
Heat to a luke-warm temperature.

101

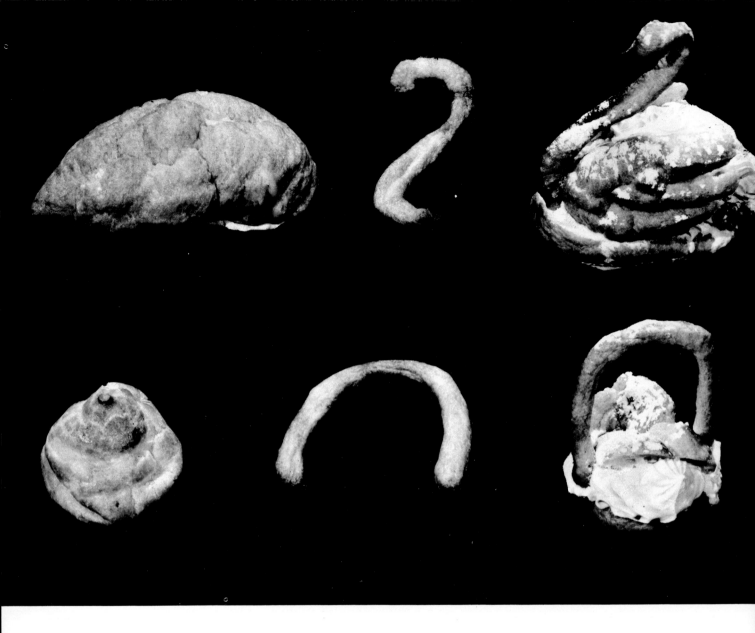

CREAM PUFFS

With your knowledge acquired in pressure control
while handling a cake decorating tube, it is possible
to work with any pliable substance and obtain any
variety of shape that you desire.

To pipe the swan, a large oblong mound is first piped
out. Fill a large cone with puff paste and cut the tip to
a ¼ inch opening. The swan neck is piped into a slight
question-mark shape. The upper third of the mound is
cut in half and after filling the cream puff with whipped
cream or ice cream, the two sections are inserted into
the mound forming the wings. The neck is then placed
into position as illustrated.

Bake in a hot oven 450 degrees. Remove when cream
puff becomes a delicate brown. After baking, the cream
puff is sliced off approximately ⅓ from the top. This
⅓ section is then cut in half and the cream puff is
filled with whipped cream or ice cream and the two
halves are placed in an angle after the handle is put
into position as illustrated.

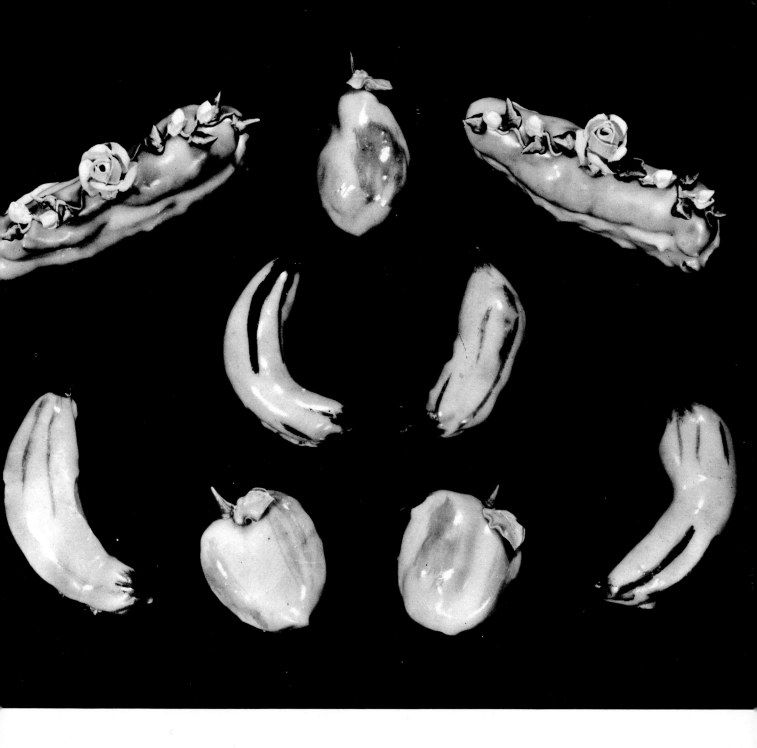

This is an example of piping fruits or any number of designs using this cream puff paste. Remember, in piping a large object do not rest the cone or tube on the pan but lift it off about ½ inch as you build up pressure. The fruits may be filled with whipped cream, custard or ice cream. Make a large cone, fill the cone with the desired filling and make a small hole at one end of the fruit. Insert the tip of your cone and apply pressure, thus filling the cream puff.

These may be placed on a rack and poured with a fondant icing, the same type we use for pouring petits fours.

The fondant icing may be colored to a pastel yellow shade. After drying, a cloth may be dipped into your coloring and rubbed over the outer edges to obtain the various color effects, a dark for the banana and a light pink for the apples and a green for the pears. By rubbing the cloth lightly over the object, you may blend in the color for a realistic effect.

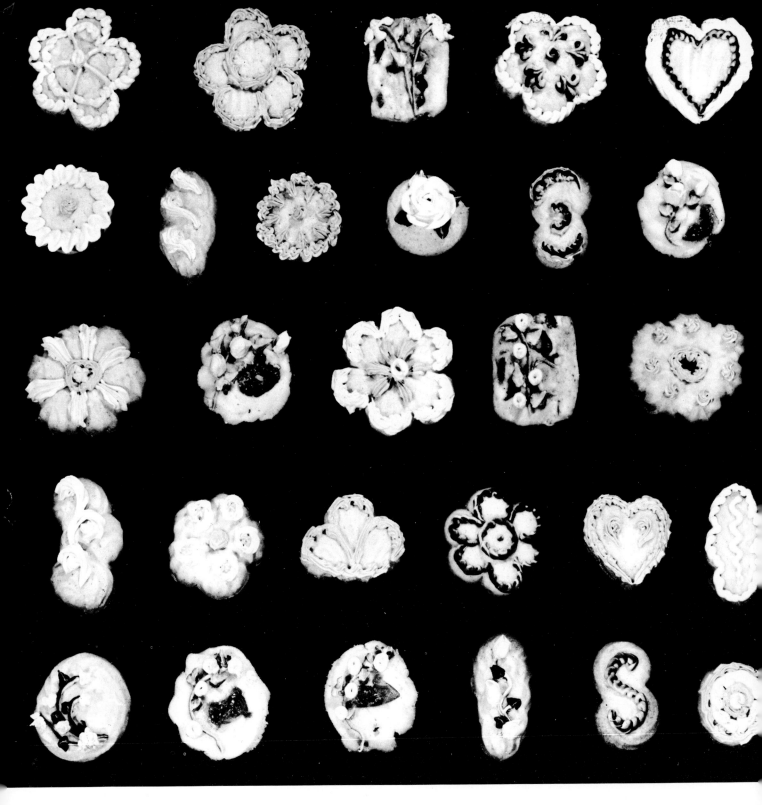

COOKIES AND THEIR DECORATIONS

After constructing a large cone, a No. 30 star tube is dropped into the cone. Using your favorite cookie batter, try piping out some small individual designs as illustrated here. After the cookies have cooled, you may use your rose nail. Put a small dot of icing on the nail. Place the cookie on top the nail and by spinning the nail in your left hand, you may use a small tube of any desired size and decorate the cookies following some of the designs illustrated here. In most cases we have used a No. 16 tube. As pressure is

applied to the tube, the nail is turned in the left hand in a counter-clockwise motion. After the design is completed, lift the cookie off the nail and place on wax paper to dry.

Much time will be saved using this method. Many intricate designs may be worked out with a minimum amount of effort. Using a variation of pastel colors and any desired decorating icing, the overall effect will be very pleasing.

CHAPTER IX

Decorating Variations

CREAM CHEESE DECORATING

Depending on the type of decorating you intend to do with cream cheese it will be necessary to vary your recipe slightly.

Allow an 8 oz. package of cream cheese to stand until it warms to room temperature. Beat at slow speed and gradually add one teaspoon of cream. Add desired coloring. If a thinner consistency is desired, add more cream. For making flowers omit cream completely.

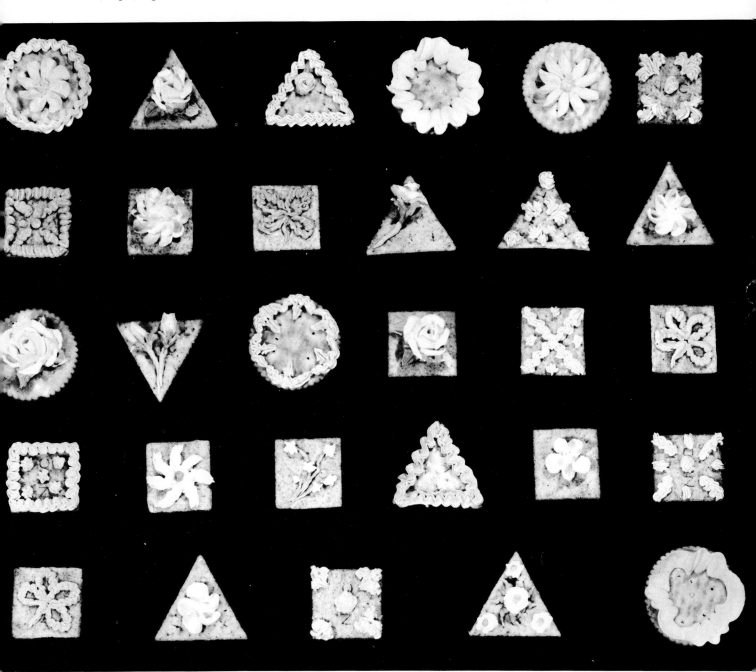

CRACKER DECORATIONS

Oval, triangular and square crackers were used for a variation of designs. A No. 16 star tube was used for most of the decorations. For the flower and ribbon border we used the No. 103 tube. Any one of your favorite spreads or mixes may be piped through this tube. Using variations of design as illustrated will certainly fascinate your guests.

DECORATED SANDWICHES

In the following designs on decorated sandwiches our idea was to show you a few simple variations of designs that may be added to any sandwich using a cream cheese mix for decorating. All of the illustrations shown were made with a No. 24 star tube. Remember, in bordering your small dainty work it is necessary to add a very light pressure as you move your tube in a back and forth and side to side motion. If your border is built up, it indicates that too much pressure is being applied. In working with small sandwiches a heavy pressure will be very obvious. Keep a light pressure on the cone as you follow around into the various border designs.

SANDWICH LOAF

For best results use day old bread. Remove crust from bread. Cut lengthwise in four slices approximately ¾ inch thick. Before adding the desired filling such as egg salad, ham, olive, etc., spread each slice with a thin coating of butter to prevent the mixture from soaking into bread. After fillings are completed, ice the entire loaf with a thin layer of cream cheese. For our loaf, we used a pastel green for the icing. A No. 30 star tube was used for the bottom and top border. This border is made by moving your tube in a side to side motion as pressure is applied. The pale pink roses and rosebuds in the spray on top, were made with a No. 103 tube. For these flowers we used cream cheese which had been whipped. Do not thin this mixture with cream because stiffer cream cheese is needed to make the petals of the rose. After decorating refrigerate until serving.

CENTERPIECE

This centerpiece is made by wrapping a grape fruit in tin foil. The olives are placed on toothpicks and are decorated in the same manner as working on a nail, by squeezing the cone and turning the toothpick, the various designs are made. A No. 16 star tube and a No. 104 tube were used to decorate these olives. The cone was filled with a well beaten cream cheese. After the olives are decorated they are placed into a colorful arrangement into the grapefruit.

Hors d'oeuvres or decorated crackers may be placed around the base of the grapefruit for an unusual centerpiece.

DECORATED HORS D'OEUVRES

As you have probably noticed while going through this book, any substance that can be beaten up to the proper consistency can be used for decorating.

In decorating hors d'oeuvres you will find fish pastes, cheeses and many other foods that you may like can be presented in a different and unusual manner. A No. 16 Star Tube and a No. 103 Tube were used for most of the designs shown in the above picture.

When decorating the hors d'oeuvre it will be easier if you place it on your decorating nail. This will allow you to turn the hors d'oeuvre as you apply pressure on the cone.

These decorations are very unusual and your guests will be amazed at the numerous designs you have created in this manner.

PEAR SLICES

Pear slices decorated with cream cheese with the use of a No. 30 star tube.

CANDLELIGHT SALAD

This salad is made up from pineapple, banana, cherry and decorated with whipping cream. So easy to make and so eye appealing.

SPLIT PINEAPPLE

Split a fresh pineapple in half and hollow out with a spoon or sharp instrument. Mix the fresh pineapple with fruit cocktail and salad dressing. A little whipping cream may be whipped up. Mix together and put back into the pineapple. The top of the pineapple is decorated with a cream cheese using a No. 30 star tube.

Molded fruit salad filled and decorated with whipped cream. The decorations on the top of the salad were made with a No. 30 star tube. The small apple blossoms were made with royal icing in pastel pink.

A colorful vegetable plate is made up of radishes, parsley, cucumbers and celery. With the use of well beaten cream cheese and your No. 30 star tube, you can finish this salad off perfectly.

MARTHA E's FROZEN DELIGHT

This particular salad was made from gelatine, lemon juice, cream cheese, mayonnaise, salt, sugar, whipped cream, chopped nuts, maraschino cherries, and fruit cocktail. After your favorite recipe is molded, it may be placed on a dish and decorated as follows; 4 bunches of frosted grapes are worked around the corners. To frost the grapes, use ½ cup sugar, and the juice from one lemon, dip grapes in lemon and sprinkle with sugar. After drying they acquire a frosty look. Do not place in refrigerator, as the sugar will melt. The parsley is then worked in around the bunches of grapes. The top of the mold is decorated with a No. 30 star tube, and three large roses made with cream cheese are placed on top. The roses are a pastel pink. The decorating was done in white, using the No. 30 star tube.

Here are a few simple dessert toppings. All were decorated using the No. 30 star tube and a heavy whipping cream.

Strawberry shortcake simply decorated.
Use whipped cream, with a No. 30 star tube.

Strawberries nestled among light green whipped cream leaves make a colorful topping. The bottom border was finished in light green also using a No. 30 star tube. The jello mold was done in pink.

CHAPTER X

Special Techniques

Lattice = Cake Top Pieces = Basket Weaving

LATTICE DESIGNS

Royal icing thinned down with egg white must be used for all types of lattice. An even, uniform flow of icing is obtained when a steady pressure is used on the cone.

LATTICE SCALLOP

A pattern approximately 8 inches high is first drawn on paper as illustrated. Use a large cone of royal icing. Cut the tip to a ¼ inch opening. Place a sheet of wax paper over this pattern and outline heavily as illustrated. After the pattern is outlined use the same tube with a circular motion to go over the outline once more. A thin line is then drawn over the pattern for the last time as illustrated. While the icing is still soft, the wax paper is lifted and placed in a curve such as the inside of a No. 10 tin can. When the royal icing dries after about 24 hours, the wax paper is peeled off the design. The lattice design is then placed on top the 6 inch corrugated circle iced in royal icing. Love-birds, dainty roses and buds may be used to decorate as illustrated.

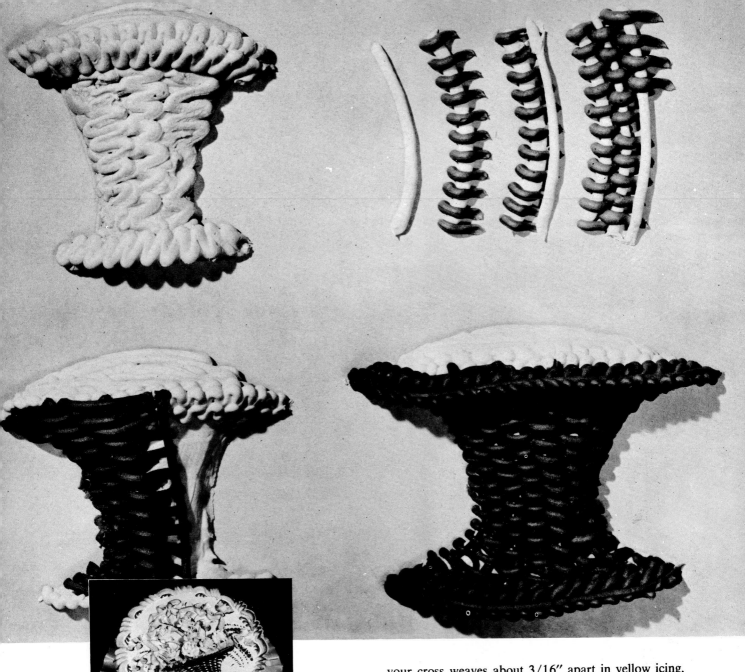

BASKET WEAVING

In constructing a woven basket of icing, the following procedure is used:

Fill a large cone with white icing using a No. 16 tube. Fill another small cone with yellow or any desired icing and cut the tip off for about a 3/16" opening. The desired shape and size of the basket is first drawn out with the small cone. Using the No. 16 tube, the basket outline is then filled in to simulate a half basket as illustrated.

Before attempting to weave the basket, we suggest you try a few practice steps as follows: Using the No. 16 tube, draw a vertical line about 3" long. Then make your cross weaves about 3/16" apart in yellow icing, using your small cone. After completing the cross weaves, make another vertical line ⅛" away from the first line. Then complete your cross weave in yellow icing starting in the center of the first cross weave. This procedure is continued across the entire basket. Study the weaving procedure closely and follow the description. After a few practice tries start weaving your basket. Once the basket is completely woven, the upper portion and the base are overpiped using the small cone in yellow.

Before filling the basket with flowers, the handle is piped on in any desired shape and the stems and leaves are then placed on using a pastel icing.

The handle may be tied with a bow, using the No. 104 tube in any desired color.

Many variations of tubes may be used in weaving a basket, but the most important thing is the proper shape and the neatness of the weaving. Plan your color scheme so that it blends in well for the particular occasion.

SCENERY PAINTING IN ICINGS

The cake is first iced in a thin layer of buttercream and then poured with a lukewarm fondant. Before painting the scene, the cake should dry for one hour. Scenery painting in icings can be practiced on corrugated cardboard circles before attempting an actual cake scene.

A thinned down boiled icing and vegetable paste colors are used for this type of painted cake top. In painting a scene such as the boat, clouds and land in background, a picture may be obtained and copied in the following manner: With a brush approximately 1½ inches in diameter, a small amount of thinned down boiled icing is placed in the skyline area. Using the brush in a back and forth motion, the skyline is painted in. With a tiny brush, place four or five small dots of blue paste color in the skyline area. Using a larger brush in a series of back and forth motions gives the skyline a blue variegated effect. A large cone of white boiled icing with a ¼ inch opening at the tip is used in a zig-zag motion at various intervals to obtain the cloud effect. Go over this cloud area with a clean brush to give it a smooth realistic look. The water area is made by piping on a thinned down white boiled icing and then adding a few drops of blue and green paste color. Then, with the use of the large brush in a series of sweeping motions, create the greenish blue water effect. Use the deeper colors for the distant water. The ship may be put in with the fill-in method or it may be outlined and then painted on with the brush as illustrated.

Before putting in the clouds and after the blue is put on, a few dots of yellow, orange and a tint of violet may be brushed right above the horizon to give a sunset effect. After practicing a few simple scenes such as these, you will see that scenery painting is simple and fast once you have acquired the technique of using the brush properly.

For the Western scene, the sky was painted in first as previously described. The mountains were piped on with a white and brown icing. Then, using a small brush, a few dots of deep colored icing were put on the crevices and then smoothed out with a larger brush. The cowboy and horse were painted on with a very small brush in deeper colored boiled icing thinned down to the consistency of oil paints.

The Halloween scene is painted in chocolate, orange and yellow. In a scene such as this, you must keep in mind the angle of the moon's shadows. This cake was bordered with individual shells using the No. 30 star tube and was overpiped in a deep color with a No. 3 tube using a question mark design.

Floral Arrangements and Cake Tops

After practicing the many variations of border work
and flower designs, we will combine these techniques
to finish the cake.

TOP DESIGN

Before placing floral arrangements on a cake, we suggest you practice first on an inverted cake or pie pan. After making your favorite cake, select a frosting to complement it. It is a good idea to contrast the cake and frosting. Using a rich frosting for a plain cake, a fluffy delicate one for a sponge type, angel food or chiffon cake.

A large number of flowers used on any cake top does not necessarily improve its appearance. A floral arrangement is the key to beautifying a cake top. No matter how realistic the flowers look, there must be a graceful

arrangement of the stems in order to place the flowers in the proper positions.

The message should be written on the cake first. It is much easier to work the stems around the inscription than to squeeze the writing in after the floral spray is completed. The most noticeable mistake made is having stiff looking stems.

Use a No. 67 leaf tube and a No. 4 tube for the stems. It is necessary to thin the icing down in order to draw your stems out without breaking. A thinner icing also helps when drawing your leaves out to a point.

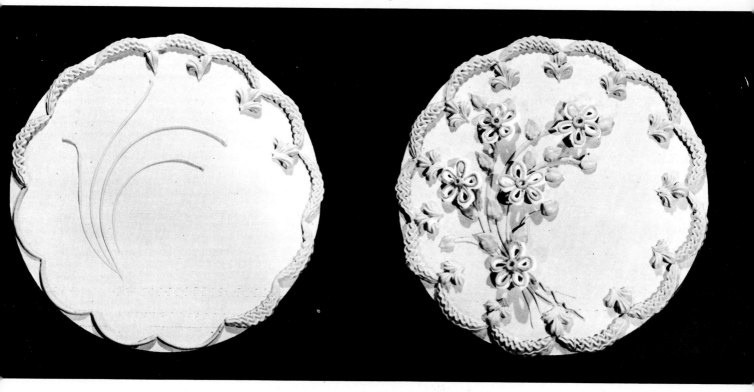

This simplified cake top was made with a No. 16 tube. Use a glass to obtain the uniform curved design. The curve is then followed with your No. 16 tube.

After working in the stems, leaves are placed on. The five flowers were made up in advance in royal icing and placed on the cake after drying.

A

B

C

D

E

F

G

H

These 8-stem arrangements may be used for many variations of cake top layouts. To obtain a curved graceful layout start with the longest stem. After this first curved line or stem is worked around the cake, the other stems are worked on from either side. These are started in opposite directions to give the stems a realistic look. The stems on cakes A and E come down to one point before going out again. This is done in order to work a small cluster of flowers in at this point. The other arrangements will be discussed in detail in later pages. Before the flowers are placed on, try working on a few leaves in their proper places as shown in Fig. G. Figure H is a very simple arrangement with five small drop flowers placed in their proper position and finished off with a cluster at the base of the spray. This flower is described in detail under *"Flowers."* As you will recall, it is made by simply squeezing and turning the tube to complete the five petals.

Illustrated above is a completed stem layout using the sweetpea and cluster arrangement.

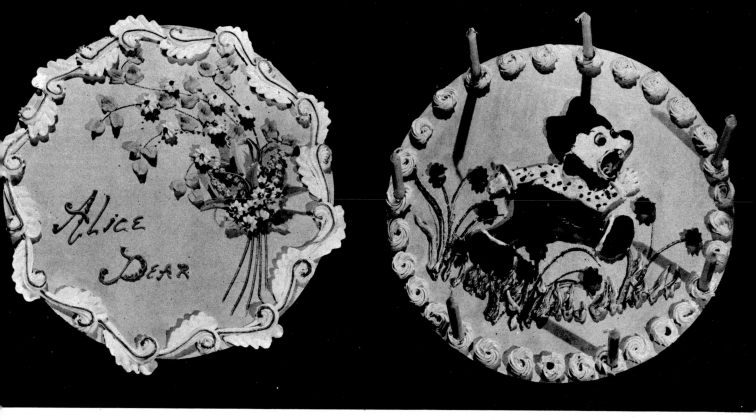

The interesting thing about this cake top is the floral arrangement. After the stems are drawn out, small leaves are then piped into place. The tiny pink flowers were made with a No. 30 tube. As you will recall, a simple squeeze and stop completes this flower.

A series of rosettes were piped around the cake with a No. 30 tube. The desired number of candles are then placed into the rosettes. The figure was put on the cake using the fill-in method as described under figure piping.

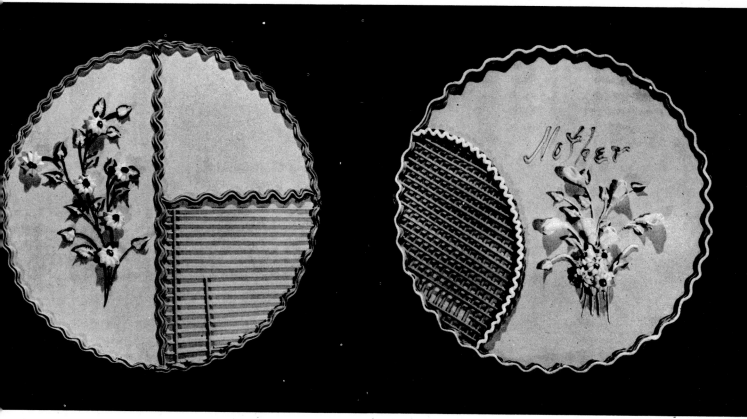

This cake border was made with a No. 16 tube. The lattice work in the lower right hand corner was completed with a No. 4 tube. After completing the stem arrangement, small drop flowers are worked into the stems using a No. 30 tube.

Before decorating this cake, a small curved outline is drawn in. The lattice work is then placed into the outline. The cake is trimmed with a No. 16 tube. A tiny stem arrangement with buds completes this simple cake.

The musical staff was made with a No. 4 tube. The border was made with a No. 16 tube held directly above the cake. The border is completed by simply squeezing and stopping and continuing all around the cake. Three simple arrangements of flowers were worked in to complete this unusual cake top.

The cake top was trimmed with a No. 16 tube using a gentle back and forth motion as you move around the outer edge of the cake. The flowers may be piped directly on the cake or be made up ahead of time on a nail in royal icing.

This cake top is trimmed with a No. 16 star tube. The border is then gone over using a No. 4 tube in a contrasting color.

Cornucopia arrangement. The cake is first trimmed with a No. 30 tube. A large cone cut to a ¼ inch opening is used to fill-in the horn's base. The base is then overpiped completing the horn effect. A small mound of icing is worked into the mouth of the horn as a fill-in. The stems and grapes were then piped in and the small tea roses were added last.

This is an 8 inch cake trimmed in a pastel green border. The stems and leaves are dark green. Three yellow jonquils make up the floral arrangement.

This is an 8 inch two layer cake iced in white. The border was trimmed in pastel pink with three dahlias completing the floral arrangement.

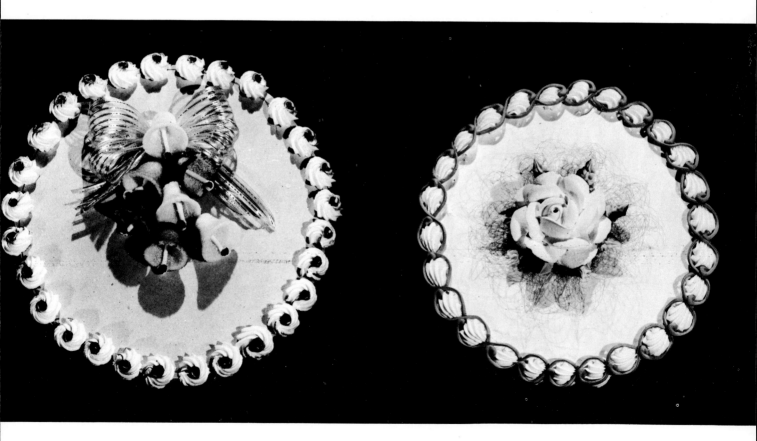

This cake is trimmed with a No. 30 tube. The cluster of bells are made with the sugar mold method. The ribbon was tied and placed in position before the bells were arranged.

For decorating this cake, pastel green netting is ruffled and worked around in a circular pattern. A pastel pink rose was placed in the middle with green leaves working out from beneath. The border is a shell border trimmed with a No. 4 tube.

This cake is trimmed with a No. 30 tube. Four tiny clusters of forget-me-nots complete the floral arrangement.

After the border is placed on, pastel pink netting was ruffled around and added in the center of the cake. A small bouquet of roses was then worked into the center.

The outer border was made with a No. 16 tube. The half circles were piped on with a No. 4 tube. Two chrysanthemums complete this cake top arrangement.

This cake was trimmed with a No. 30 tube. A dainty ribbon was placed in the center of the cake. A small amount of icing is piped in the center of the ribbon and sweet peas, drop flowers and rose buds were used to complete this bouquet.

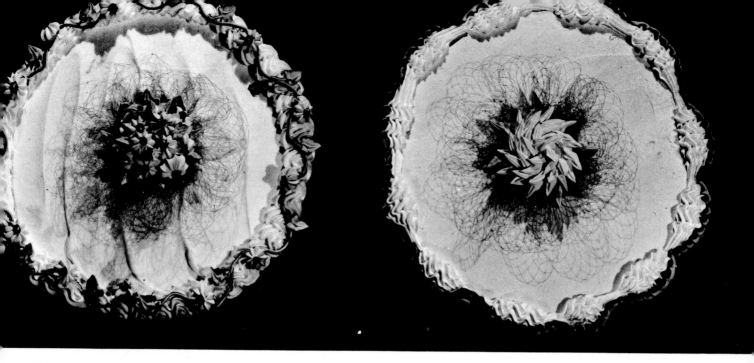

The outer border was piped on with a No. 30 tube. A small vine was worked around the border and completed by working in tiny drop flowers and leaves. Pastel pink netting and drop flowers complete the bouquet in the center.

A No. 30 tube was used for the outer border. Pastel green netting was used for the center bouquet. A delicate pink Mum was placed in the center of the bouquet.

A small mound of icing is placed in the center of the cake. The sweetpeas cover the mound and the stems and leaves are then worked around. A small ribbon and bow are then tied at the base of the cluster.

This cake was trimmed with a No. 30 tube. Three small clusters of roses and sweet peas complete this dainty arrangement.

This cake was divided into eight sections. The border was completed with a No. 16 tube and the fluted edge worked in with a No. 103 tube. The graceful effect is obtained by the proper stem arrangement. Three pink roses are used for the floral design.

This cake was trimmed with a No. 30 tube. Lilies of the valley, sweet peas and drop flowers were used in this floral arrangement. The bouquet is then tied with a dainty bow.

This border was made of white icing using the No. 30 tube and the No. 104 tube for the fluted edge. A small mound of icing was piped into the center of the cake before working out the floral arrangement.

The stems and leaves are placed on after piping out a mound of icing in the center of the cake. Orange blossoms, roses and lilies of the valley make up this floral arrangement.

SIMPLIFIED CAKE TOP SHELL MOTIF

A very effective cake top can be produced in a series of simple moves. The cake is first divided into four equal parts. If you are not too steady at freehand, use a glass or any other circular pattern to draw in the four half circles. The half circles are then overpiped using a No. 30 star tube. A steady even pressure must be applied as you move the cone in a smooth rhythmical motion finishing each design without pausing. A small rosette is piped in the center of the cake with four small shells completing the design. The cake is then finished off with a shell border.

DAISY CAKE TOP

Here is the procedure used in constructing the garland border. Fill a cone with white icing using a No. 16 star tube. With a very light pressure, move the tube back and forth slightly increasing the pressure and then relaxing pressure again forming the garland. After this is completed around the entire cake, a No. 104 tube is used for the fluted edge on the outside of the garland. This cone should be filled with a pastel pink icing. Pressing the heavy side of the tube to the cake and with the small end standing out and up slightly, start the pressure. As pressure is applied, move the tube in a series of back and forth motions following the edge of the garland. This garland is then overpiped in white icing with a No. 16 star tube. Then go over one more time using a small cone with a No. 4 tube and a delicate pink icing completing the border. After the stems are placed on the cake, a few leaves are put into position and the daisies which were made up ahead of time in royal icing are placed at various angles to give the cake a lifelike effect.

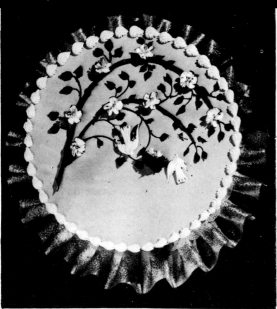

TWELVE INCH CAKE WITH AMERICAN BEAUTY ROSE SPRAY

This is a fine example using few flowers. With the proper arrangement, a beautiful cake top is obtained. A No. 199 tube was used for the shell effect on the borderline of the cake.

SIMPLIFIED FLORAL ARRANGEMENT WILD FLOWER SPRAY

The stems are piped on using the No. 4 tube. Small dainty leaves are then piped on using the No. 67 leaf tube. In arranging the tiny wild flowers, face them in various directions giving them a more realistic look. The cake is finished with a simple shell border.

ROSE MOTIF WITH CLUSTER

The Cake is bordered with a Reverse Shell.

ROSE SPRAY TOP

Illustrating roses properly arranged. Three roses and four tiny buds complete this ten inch cake top. Outer shell border is completed with No. 30 tube in delicate yellow.

SPRING MOTIF

A spring cake with yellow jonquils iced with a pastel green. The border is finished off with a ribbon swag using the No. 104 tube. Long narrow leaves are piped on using the No. 67 leaf tube.

POPPY CAKE

For an unusual effect this cake was iced with a thin layer of butter-cream and then covered by pouring lukewarm fondant over it. The shell border is completed with a No. 30 star tube, and the fluted edge is worked in pastel green using a No. 104 tube.

FALL CAKE

You can start the fall season with one of its loveliest flowers, the Dahlia. The Dahlia is made with the use of a No. 104 tube and royal icing. Colors may be used as desired, pink, red, yellow, white or a deep purple. Using deep shades, these colors blend together to give an endless variety of color effects. The flower is described in detail under "*Flowers*." But we will show you again the various steps. In completing the Cake Top, the stems and leaves are placed on first. In arranging the flowers, be sure to pipe small cones on the under side of the flower and place it slightly on its side giving the flower a realistic look. The rope border is almost self-explanatory. A No. 30 star tube is employed in the border as explained and illustrated under "*Borders*."

ROSE BASKET DESIGN

The detail of the basket and border of this 12-inch cake top are explained under *"Special Techniques."* The basket is woven in purple and white with pink roses and buds completing the design. A No. 104 tube was used to achieve a ribbon swag border on the outer edge. The flower portion of the cake was finished off with a shell border using a pastel green icing. It is customary to write on a cake top such as this, and here is an idea that has genuine appeal. Obtain some small gift cards such as used by florists, and write your personal message. The card is then placed in the basket in an upright position.

RAG DOLL CAKE

A doll cake is very attractive for little girl's Birthday parties, yet relatively simple to make. To form the doll's head, first fill your decorating cone with flesh-pink icing. Use your No. 4 TUBE, holding it at a 45° angle to the surface. Apply pressure on your cone, lift-up ¼″, continuing pressure until ball is complete. For the doll's body, follow the above procedure, but elongate the ball by bringing the cone towards you, while you apply pressure.

Two-tone dress ruffles are made by stripping your decorating cone with deep coloring, placed on the same side of the cone as the narrowest end of DECORATING TUBE. Pastel icing should be inserted in the remainder of the cone. Lower ruffle is completed first. Large end of the No. 104 TUBE must touch cake, then squeeze cone and move along with a slight side to side motion to gain fluted effect. Bonnet is made in the same manner. Star flower border is made with pink icing and a No. 30 STAR TUBE. Hold cone perpendicular, apply pressure, stop and lift up.

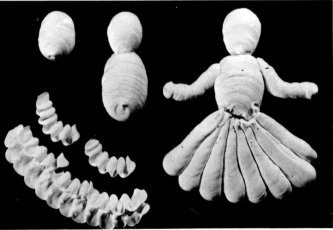

Fan-like skirt is made by forming separate strips, starting from the bottom of the cake and working upwards towards the body, gradually decreasing pressure. Arms are formed as shown, starting at the shoulders. HAIR should be made with a yellow icing and a No. 4 TUBE, using a series of criss-cross motions. Eyes and nose are "X's" made with a No. 4 TUBE and red icing. Mouth, collar and buttons are made with the same icing and TUBE.

130

DRUM CAKE

This colorful 8″ cake decorated as a drum is sure to delight any youngster! Very deep colors are recommended—we chose red and yellow. The two bands at the top and bottom of the cake were made with a No. 124 ROSE TUBE.

Fill your decorating cone with yellow icing and insert your No. 124 TUBE. Hold cone flat against the side of the cake and using a steady, even pressure move along the upper edge until the band is complete. Use this same procedure for the lower band. Pipe criss-cross sections that hold bands together with a No. 4 TUBE, using red icing.

Drumsticks are made with a No. 4 TUBE, starting pressure at the top of the drumstick and gradually decreasing. Finish drumstick tip off with a dot of icing. The drumsticks can be made directly on the cake or they may be made in ROYAL ICING on waxed paper and after drying, placed on the cake top.

Rosettes are made with a No. 30 STAR TUBE. Hold the cone perpendicular in your right hand, using left hand as a guide. Squeeze gently and lift up. Candles are placed in the center of the rosettes while they are still soft.

THE ORCHID CAKE

Because the orchid is made in six sections and then put together, it must be made in royal icing. This is explained in detail under *"Flowers."* The cake top may be worked with only one flower, or a few roses and buds may be worked in as shown in the illustrated cake top. The fluted edge border is worked in a delicate purple and white icing.

CHAPTER XII

Special Occasion Cakes

There is no better time to show off your newly acquired cake decorating skill than on the special holidays.

MOTHER'S DAY HAT

This is an 8 inch layer cake placed on a 10 inch cardboard base. Before placing the cake on the 10 inch base the top is cut down at a slight angle to give the cake a simulated hat effect. The cardboard is then iced in a pastel green icing. After the base is iced, a 2 inch netting is worked around the cardboard base. The 8 inch layer that has been cut down is then iced in a pastel green and placed on the 10 inch cardboard base. The hat is trimmed with a No. 16 star tube. Any desired flower or floral arrangement may be applied.

FATHER'S DAY HAT

Two 8 inch layers are placed on a 10 inch cardboard. Make sure that your second layer is flat on top. Fill a No. 16 star tube with yellow icing. Starting at the top outer edge, use a series of back and forth motions approximately ½ inch in width. As you move the tube along in a steady even movement and after completing the circumference of the cake, move the tube in ½ inch and start another series until the entire top is completed. The same procedure is followed on the side of the cake. The hat band is made using the same tube with a contrasting colored icing. Leave about ¾ inch space for the hat band. The hat rim is trimmed in the same manner starting at the inner edge and working out. "Dad" is written using the No. 16 star tube and a contrasting color.

VALENTINE'S DAY CAKE

This is a two-layer 9 inch cake iced in a white boiled icing and trimmed with a No. 30 star tube using a deep red color. Small candied hearts are placed to simulate a heart pierced by an arrow.

FLAG CAKE

We use a two layer oblong cake iced in white icing as a beginning for the flag. First mark out the area of the blue field. Then cover this field with a side to side motion using a cone of blue icing with a No. 16 tube. The next step is to add the red stripes. Use a large cone filled with red icing and a No. 30 star tube. Draw out the top and bottom red stripes along the edges of the cake using a very fine back and forth movement. Next draw out the center red stripe extending to the right

from the bottom of the blue field. Using these three stripes as guides, add the remaining four red stripes spaced appropriately as illustrated. The six white stripes are then drawn out between the red stripes using white icing and following the same method. A cone of white icing with a No. 16 star tube is then used to add the 48 white stars in the blue field and to trim the cake as illustrated. This handsome cake is very easy to prepare and makes an outstandingly effective centerpiece.

UNCLE SAM'S HAT

The children will enjoy a cake decorated to simulate Uncle Sam's Hat. Three seven inch layers were placed on top of each other. Invert the top layer in order to make it flat on top. Ice a 10 inch circle with white icing. Place the three seven inch layers on the 10 inch cardboard. The entire cake is then iced with white icing. The hat is trimmed using a No. 30 star tube and red icing. The band is made with a blue icing using the No. 30 star tube. The stars are piped on the hat after outlining the stars and filling in with a No. 16 star tube. The rim of the hat is trimmed in blue icing using a No. 16 star tube.

CONFIRMATION CAKE

Here is a 10 inch layer cake iced in white with a full garland border at the top and a shell border with edging for the base. Four small mounds of icing were placed on the cake's edge an equal distance apart. Small stems and dainty leaves were then worked into each mound. Dainty drop flowers made with the No. 190 tube were then placed on the clusters, giving the cake an unusual bouquet effect. The bible is made by the sugar mold method.

FOOTBALL CAKE

The football is made with a small Easter Egg mold using the sugar mold method. The cake is trimmed in a pastel yellow with a No. 30 star tube. Granulated sugar was colored green by placing a little color in the sugar and mixing. The sugar was then sprinkled on the cake top. Lines to simulate a football field were piped in with white icing.

FIRST ANNIVERSARY CAKE

This is an 8 inch cake trimmed with a simple border and three tiny sugar bells worked in a series on the side of the cake. These bells were made by using the sugar bell method described in detail in this book. The bells were outlined in royal icing and dipped in silver dragees (small silver candied balls). The rose was made in royal icing and a 5 inch candle placed in the center of the rose.

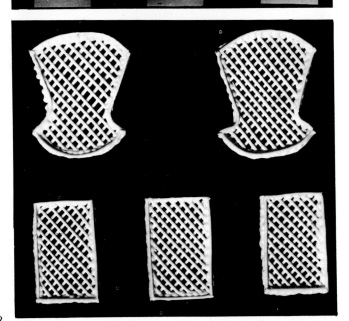

BABY SHOWER CAKE

For this particular cake, we used a 3 layer, 10 inch cake iced in white. After inscription is written, a reverse shell border is worked around the top edge and base of cake.

5 small mounds of icing are then placed at equal distances apart on edge of cake with tiny stems piped on to simulate a climbing vine. Any type of small flower may be used for clusters; if tiny roses are preferred use the No. 104 rose tube.

Draw and cut pattern for baby's crib as illustrated. Actual size will be approximately 3 inches by 2 inches. Fill small cone with royal icing and insert No. 4 tube. Place sheet of waxed paper over pattern and work lattice design over each section. Outline each with small border. Allow 12 hours to dry.

Place crib end on waxed paper. Fill cone with thinned down royal icing, spreading it lightly over sides of two rectangle pieces. Attach and insert 2nd crib end. To form base, run icing along 4 sides of 3rd rectangle piece and place it against bottom of crib. Set on warm oven 1 hour to dry before decorating.

Pipe swans on both sides of crib with pastel royal icing as trimming.

EASTER CAKE

The flower pot and flowers may be made up in advance, by using ROYAL ICING and working on wax paper. After drying for 12 hours, flowers may be lifted from the paper and placed on the cake.

When working directly on the cake, draw an outline or cut a stencil of a flower pot. Fill-in, as illustrated using a No. 16 TUBE on a cone filled with yellow icing. After stems are drawn with a No. 4 TUBE, flowers are made in the following manner:

To make top border. Fill cone with pink icing and insert No. 199 TUBE. Use gentle side to side motion similar to SWAY BORDER.

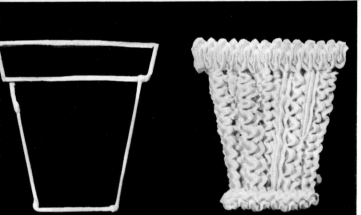

 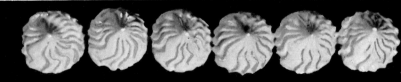

Spring flowers can be made in various pastel shades, using a No. 103 TUBE. Make flower base (which is a flat petal lying down) by placing widest end of tubes directly on the cake, with narrow end slightly raised. Squeeze cone and pivot tube slightly to complete base. Start first petal directly on center of base, holding cone at 45° angle. Squeeze and lift slightly. Then relax pressure and bring cone down toward cake. Place petals at a slight angle to center petal. Leaves are drawn on with a green icing, using a No. 67 TUBE. Two clusters of spring flowers may be placed on the sides of the cake.

Button border, use a No. 199 TUBE. hold the cone at a slight angle to cake, apply pressure and move away from the cake ¼ inch while rotating the cone slightly. Discontinue pressure to break off icing neatly.

BALLERINA CAKE

The star border around the side of the cake was made with a No. 199 tube in a pastel pink icing. The border is trimmed with a small cone using a No. 3 tube. The ballerina dancers were made using the fill in method and described in detail under *Figure Piping*.

SPACE MAN CAKE

An eye appealing cake for any young boy. The outer border is made with the No. 199 tube in a pastel blue and trimmed in bright red, using the No. 3 tube. The rocket ship and the space man were piped out using the fill in method and are described in detail under *Figure Piping*. Bright red and yellow colors were used.

PATRIOTIC MOTIF CAKE

To make the flags, draw the design on white cardboard and cut out. Following this pattern, draw two flags, one to the right side and the other reversed to the left. Fill two cones with royal icing using red in one and white in the other. The icing should be thinned down to insure smooth flow. Cut the tip of the cones to approximately ⅛ inch opening. Place the flag pattern on a pan or any other flat surface. Cover with waxed paper. The 13 stripes are piped along the entire pattern. The blue background for the stars is piped over the striped upper corner and smoothed out slightly with a small knife or brush. Using a small cone with a fine tip, the 48 stars are then piped in. Twelve to twenty-four hours are required for these flags to dry. Peel off the waxed paper and place the flags on the cake. The flag pole is then piped in place. The eagle may be piped on the cake or made with the use of the sugar mold method. To make the rope border use red and white icing, described in detail under *Borders*.

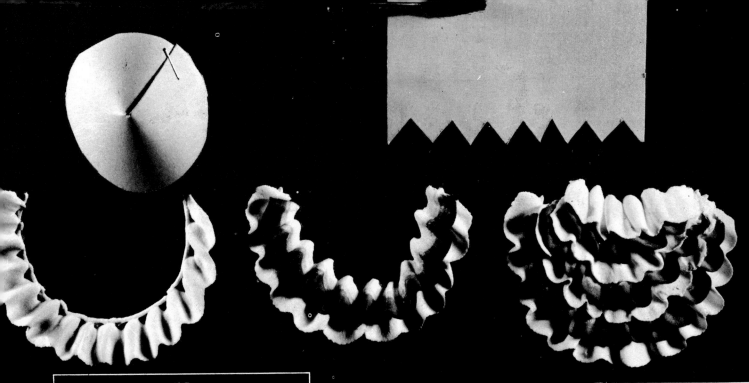

THE DOLL CAKE

The illustrations are almost self-explanatory, but we will briefly outline the procedure to make it more clearly understood. The finished cake contains a complete little doll that may be dressed in doll clothing after the cake has been eaten. Use the doll in any cake. Here, we use a torte cake.

The unusual scalloped effect in the skirt, is made with the use of a cardboard comb.

The comb is moved in a slight up and down motion as you work it around the cake. For best results, this scalloped effect should be started at the base of the cake.

For the upper portion of the dress, thin down a small amount of delicate pink boiled or royal icing. Paint the top portion of the dress with a brush. For our illustrations, we used a strapless type gown. The bustle or ruffle effect in the next step is made with a No. 104 rose tube. The lower ruffle is completed first. With the large end of the tube touching the cake and the narrow end standing down and out, begin squeezing the tube and moving along the curve with a slight back and forth motion. This gives the fluted edge effect. A very dainty effect may be obtained by alternating the ruffles; first a white and then a pink ruffle. In finishing off the dress, a small pink flower was placed between all the lower ruffles. A sash with bow and streamers flowing down the side of the dress is piped on in delicate pink icing. The hat may be made of gumpaste, but we suggest the use of paper to eliminate the bother of making gumpaste. Cut out a 2 inch circle; make one cut in to the center of the circle and overlap the cut edges about ½ inch and staple. The hat may be painted with a thinned down pink icing. This doll may be used for a birthday cake or wedding cake. In the latter case, the dolls should be dressed in colors matching the bridesmaids.

143

VALENTINE HEART CAKE

This uniquely beautiful Valentine cake is made the following way: Ice your cake with white frosting. The heart can be drawn with a sharp stick or can be cut as a stencil, and outlined directly on the cake. The fluted edge effect is made by placing your No. 103 TUBE in decorating cone stripped with deep red color and filled with pink icing. Move the tube back and forth as you follow the heart outline. Small hearts are made by drawing directly on the cake or by cutting a stencil and outlining them with a No. 4 TUBE.

The drop flower border is illustrated in steps and under Borders.

Ribbon border is made with No. 103 TUBE, placing the large end of the tube directly on the cake. Small end should stand slightly out. Apply light pressure, as too much will cause the ribbon to ripple, instead of being smooth. Use one long, then three short strokes, as you move around the outer edge of the cake with your decorating tube.

CLOWN CAKES

Floral and border designs do not appeal to children, but this 10 inch cake decorated as a drum is sure to delight any youngster. The two bands at the top and bottom of the cake, were made with a No. 124 rose tube. Very deep colors are recommended on a cake of this type. We used red and yellow. Fill a cone with yellow icing and use a No. 124 tube. Hold the tube against the side of the cake using a steady even pressure, move along the upper edge until the band is complete. The same procedure is followed for the lower band. The criss-cross sections that hold the bands together are piped on in a bright red icing with a No. 4 tube. The figure piping of the clown is described in detail under *Figure Piping*. Instead of piping the clown lying flat on the cake, a more realistic effect is brought about by working the clowns into the comical positions as shown.

HAPPY NEW YEAR CAKE

An eye appealing cake top to be used for the New Year. "Happy New Year" is first written on the cake in a very bright color. The bells are made by the sugar mold method. A small amount of royal icing is piped around the edges of the bells which are then dipped into silver dragees. The shell border is placed on the outside of the cake using a No. 30 star tube. The holly and berries are piped on in deep green and bright red. The white streamers and bow tying the bells are made with a No. 104 tube.

146

GRADUATION CAKE DESIGN

First we will complete the border. Divide the cake into 8 equal parts. The next step is to complete the lattice work making sure to keep the lines an equal distance apart. In order to draw a straight line, it is necessary to lift the tube about ½ inch above the cake as you move it along in a smooth even line. The lattice work is completed as shown. The sweetpeas may be made right on the cake top or you may make them up ahead of time on waxed paper and then place them on the cake top after they are dry. The making of the sweetpea is described in detail under *Flowers*. The diploma that completes the cake top is made of gumpaste. The recipe is given in detail under *Special Techniques*. The gumpaste was rolled to about 1/16 of an inch in thickness. With a sharp instrument, cut a piece 5x8 inches and then roll it into the shape of a diploma. Use 3 sweetpeas to a cluster. The leaves are then piped in.

VALENTINE HEART CAKE

Here is a uniquely beautiful Valentine cake that can be made very quickly without the use of a mold. The first step is to cut a heart of cardboard. In this case we used a 6½ x 5½ inch heart. Using this for a pattern, trace heart on waxed paper. The next step is to take a cone of royal icing and cut the tip to an opening of ¼ inch. Begin squeezing strongly on the cone and make an outline of the heart on waxed paper. This outline should stand about ⅛ inch high. We will now prepare the fondant for the candy hearts.

 Recipe: ½ lb. Fondant
     2 tablespoons powdered sugar
     Heat fondant to 160 degrees. Remove from heat and add powdered sugar. Mix in well. Add red paste color and a few drops of oil of anise. Pour the hot fondant into the outlined heart. Allow to stand 3 minutes. Move the waxed paper to prevent sticking. When fondant is cool, peel waxed paper from hearts.

After hearts are made, decorate as illustrated.

LAMB CAKE

After baking cake in lamb mold, allow it to cool completely before frosting.

Use Butter Cream or Boiled Frosting to ice cakes. Spoon a small portion in bowl, thin slightly with water and tint pink. With a small paint brush, brush heart-shaped mask over eyes and nose of the lamb. Brush inner part of lamb's ears with pink frosting. Feet are trimmed with No. 3 tube and pink frosting. Body is decorated with white frosting, using No. 16 Star tube. Start with neck, drawing tube in short, curved motion—one line in one direction, next line in opposite direction. Cover entire surface following the contour of the lamb's body using this method.

Use royal icing for decorating. Eyes and nose are made with No. 3 tube and dark blue icing. Flower necklace is made up of small chrysanthemums in various pastel colors. Form leaves, drop flowers, daisies, jonquils and tiny chrysanthemums, following methods previously described in this book.

Arrange bed of pale green tinted coconut on top of large cake stand. Place decorated lamb in center and scatter spring flowers over the coconut.

WASHINGTON'S BIRTHDAY CAKE

A cherry tree and hatchet here symbolizes our first president's birthday. A simple shell border is first placed around the cake. The cherries are made up of marzipan and dipped in syrup. The marzipan is explained in detail under "*Candy Making*." To get the brown color for the tree and the axe, the inside of the cone is brushed with a brown paste color before the icing is put in the cone. Ice the cake in white. The tree and the axe were made ahead of time with royal icing.

EASTER LILY CAKE

This 10 inch cake top is iced with a pale yellow icing. After the inscription is written, the shell border is worked around the cake and edged with a fine cone of yellow icing. The stems are then gracefully arranged, and long narrow leaves are worked into the stem arrangement. Easter lilies are made up ahead of time.

CAKE WITH CROSS

This cake may be used for Easter, Confirmation or other religious occasions. The completed floral spray has only four flowers. Placing their leaves in the proper place and adding a few tiny blue forget-me-nots gives the floral spray a graceful look. The cross is made using the sugar mold method. The beads are simply dots of brown icing.

MOTHER'S DAY CAKE

Sure to delight her! Frost a 2-layer cake with white frosting. Borders can be done in delicate pink.

Top zig-zag Border. Insert No. 16 TUBE and hold TUBE at a 45° angle. Rest Tube lightly on the cake. Start an even pressure on the cone and as you move along, use short side to side motion.

Bottom border. See drop flower border illustrated in steps under Borders. Flower borders are made for bottom borders with No. 190 Tube by simply squeezing bag and twisting wrist.

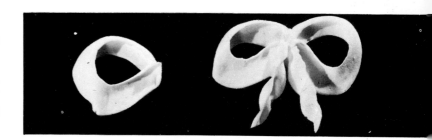

Bow is made with a No. 103 TUBE, using the motion of a figure 8, as pressure is applied to bag.

Flowers are made in various pastel colors. If made in advance, use ROYAL ICING—place flowers on wax paper and allow 12 hours to dry. Insert No. 30 STAR TUBE in decorating cone filled with white icing. Rest TUBE on waxed paper or cake (if using BUTTER CREAM) and squeeze. Relax pressure and lift up. Spot sheet of paper or cake with large white dots. Insert No. 3 TUBE and fill cone with pink or blue icing. Touch TUBE to center of dot, squeeze, relax pressure and stop. Continue making these little points around the entire center until flower is completely filled in.

HALLOWEEN CAKE

"Trick or treaters" will be delighted with this special Halloween treat! And you'll be pleased with the simple way it can be prepared. Frost a two layer cake with orange icing, using rather thick icing on the top of the cake. A spatula is used to make the grooves, or ribbed effect to simulate a pumpkin. The pumpkin face may be drawn in with a sharp stick or a tooth pick. It is then filled in with deep colored icing, using a No. 4 TUBE. The stem is piped on using the No. 30 STAR TUBE . . . No. 4 TUBE is used for pumpkin outlines on the sides of the cake.

HALLOWEEN "PLACE-CARD" CLOWNS

Individual place card cakes are perfect for Halloween parties! These attractive cakes are easily made, see Cup Cakes illustrated previously. Write place cards and insert in clown's hand. Witch Cake "Place-Cards" are made by using similar method, and decorating cup-cake with darker icing.

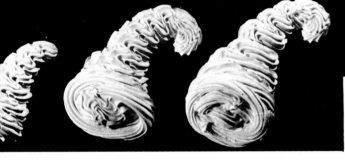

THANKSGIVING CAKE

Drop a No. 30 TUBE in cone filled with yellow icing. Place tube on cake holding cone at 45° angle. With steady, continuous pressure move the tube in a broad back and forth fashion. Build up broad end of the horn with another layer of frosting applied directly over the first, but this time make the horn as long as you want it and shape a gentle curve toward the narrow end. Go over the entire horn with a third covering of frosting applied the same way to give realistic depth to horn. Try all of these designs on a practice base, cookie or pie tin, before applying to the cake.

Button border is made with Straw colored icing and the No. 199 TUBE. Hold the cone at a slight angle to cake, apply pressure and move away from the cake ¼ inch while rotating the cone slightly. Discontinue pressure to break off icing neatly.

To make Bottom Border use No. 199 TUBE and Deep Tan icing. Follow steps under Sway Borders. See Borders.

To make grape clusters, drop a No. 4 TUBE in a cone filled with Green or Purple Icing. Hold cone at a 45° angle, apply pressure. Lift cone up slightly, then ease off on the pressure. Form an outline of these very tiny shells in the shape of a grape cluster. Fill the center of the cluster with a mound of frosting as shown in the fifth step and continue shaping the grapes over this built-in mound. Have 10 or 12 clusters of grapes varying in size and color from large to small, spilling out of the horn of plenty.

To make leaves, drop a No. 67 TUBE in cone and add green icing. To make tiny leaves, touch practice pan with tube held at 45° angle and apply a small amount of pressure. At the halfway mark release pressure and continue moving tube along, lifting tube up from pan to draw the little leaf out to the point. For a larger leaf, more pressure is applied.

155

HOLLY WREATH AND CANDLE

To make the wreath, a circle of icing about ½ inch high and 1 inch wide is piped on the cake. This forms the base of the wreath. A leaf tube is then placed in a cone that has first been brushed with green paste color and filled with green icing. This will result in a very bright Christmas green. The leaves are piped around the circle of icing. The ribbon and bow are placed on in white icing using a No. 104 tube. To make the candle, use a cone cut ¼ inch at the tip and filled with the desired colored icing. The candle is formed by squeezing the cone with a steady pressure and moving along slowly. The flame is piped in with a small cone of yellow icing. The border is made with a No. 16 star tube and is explained in detail under *Borders*.

NEW YEAR'S CAKE

This festive New Year's cake is sure to be the topic of your holiday party. CHAMPAGNE GLASS may be drawn directly on the cake with a sharp pointed instrument or by cutting a stencil and tracing the outline. Fill-in outline with a No. 16 STAR TUBE. Numerals, horn and streamers are drawn with your No. 4 TUBE.

Top drop flower border is piped in delicate pink icing, using your No. 30 TUBE. Fill cone half-full and hold it perpendicular to the edge of the cake. Apply gentle pressure, move TUBE ¼″ from cake. Start rotating decorating cone and increase pressure, then relax pressure while continuing circular motion of cone to break flower off neatly.

Bottom sway border is made with the No. 30 STAR TUBE, holding the cone at a 45° angle. Rest tube lightly on cake and start moving along with a gentle side to side motion, continuing a steady even pressure on your decorating cone. Use your left hand as a guide.

POINSETTIA CAKE

Frost with white icing, then use the No. 3 tube to pipe on the spray in green royal icing. Next, add leaves, then flowers in red royal icing, with yellow centers. The border is colorfully added with red royal icing. Script may be done in yellow or red, with ribbon in light green.

A CAKE FOR CHRISTMAS

The Santa Claus head is made using the sugar mold method. The entire mold is dropped out in pink sugar. After 2 hours of drying, the sugar mold may be trimmed with royal icing. Santa's hat is piped on using a deep red and trimmed in white. The eyebrows, beard and whiskers are also piped on in white using a No. 4 tube. These may be made up ahead of time. The wreath around the cake is made with deep green leaves and small red dots to simulate the holly berries.

CHRISTMAS TREE CAKE

The unique thing about this cake decoration is that the trees actually stand up. To make the base for these trees, use a small paper cone or an ice cream cone. With a No. 67 leaf tube filled with deep green icing, the cone is covered as illustrated starting at the base and working up. After the tree is completed, the various colored lights may be worked in by using dots of bright colors. The trees may also be dusted slightly with cornstarch to give them a snowy look.

CHAPTER XIII

Wedding Cakes

The average amateur decorator would probably not consider attempting a complicated project as decorating a wedding cake. If you have followed the simple steps in border work and flower technique you should realize by now that all these simplified designs may be easily used for a wedding cake. You can decorate your wedding cakes as completely and as beautifully as the ones shown here by following the instructions given in the previous chapters.

All of our cakes illustrated on the following pages are iced in either buttercream or poured with a fondant. Most of the decorating is done in boiled icing. A few have been done in buttercream. The ingredients used in a wedding cake can be your own favorite mix or one of the many ready-mixes. We prefer a very light mix. Each tier is normally baked in three layers with buttercream between each layer. Each tier is iced separately and placed upon the preceding tier.

The old idea of decorating a wedding cake entirely in white icing is giving way to the use of pastels. Depending on the colors the bride or attendants are wearing, the same pastel colors can be worked into the wedding cake design.

VALENTINE'S DAY WEDDING

This is a three-tiered wedding cake made from a 12, 10 and a 6 inch cake. Each tier is made up of 3 layers and was iced in a white icing.

Very simple borders were used to decorate this cake and are illustrated in steps under *Border Work*. An interesting idea that may be carried out here is to have your florist make up 3 dainty nosegays. They are placed on the side of the cake between the first and second tier. Your florist may also prepare the white heart with ruffled netting, tiny pink roses worked around either side of the heart. After placing this on the top tier with royal icing, small icing flowers are worked around the base.

The candle holders were made by placing two large candles in a regular candle holder, the smaller the better. These are placed on a sheet of waxed paper and covered with royal icing. Small tea roses which have been made up ahead of time and allowed to dry are then placed on this mound of icing. A small green stem is worked around the candle and tiny rose buds are placed on the stem.

SWEET PEA BOUQUET

This is a 10 inch and a 6 inch cake. Each cake is made up of three layers. The cake was iced in a white boiled icing. A spatula knife dipped into warm water was used to get a smooth finish in the icing. White ribbon with pink netting were ruffled and stuck to a cake tray. The cake was then placed on the ruffled edging. A large star tube with a delicate pink icing was used to trim all of the borders illustrated in this picture.

The bottom border is a simple series of back and forth movements as you continue around the cake. The next border is a simple rosette with a silver dragee placed in the center. The inside border, at the bottom of the 6 inch layer, is made by simply squeezing and stopping as you move away from the cake. The side border on the top tier was made by a simple series of squeezing and stopping.

These tiny individual stars are placed into a drop design. The top border is made using the same tube in a series of small back and forth movements as you move around the cake. The sweet pea bouquets may be made up ahead of time. After drying they are placed on the cake by adding a small amount of icing and placing in position.

The sweet peas were made on a sheet of waxed paper in pink and white royal icing. After drying they are placed in the center of a small circle of ruffled pink netting.

A small curve of wire was used to form the arch over the bride and groom. The wire is placed flat on waxed paper and covered with royal icing. The ruffled netting is then stuck to the royal icing. After this dries, it is placed in an upright position over the bride and groom. Using royal icing for the base, tiny rosebuds may be worked around the archway.

161

LILY OF THE VALLEY WEDDING CAKE

The unique thing about this wedding cake is the tiered arrangement. Realizing that the average housewife does not have large pans needed for a big wedding cake, the following procedure may be followed. Three 8 inch layer cakes are used for the base tier. A 10 inch cake is then placed on top of these. The last tier is made from a 6 inch cake. Each tier is made up of three layers. Because all of these borders are illustrated and explained in detail under *Border Work*, we will not go into detail on the various borders; but you will notice they are all simple.

The flowers used for this cake are chrysanthemums and are made up ahead of time with a No. 16 tube using royal icing. The ribbon and netting may be ruffled together and stitched with needle and thread. After putting the ribbon into position, a small mound of icing is piped on and the bouquet of flowers is then worked in. A small opening may be cut into the top tier of your cake large enough to insert a narrow glass. Using this glass, your florist may furnish you with the necessary amount of flowers and the illustrated floral arrangement may be copied.

162

FLORAL BOUQUET

All the borders on this cake were made with a No. 30 tube. The tube is held at a slight angle on the edge of the cake, and simply by squeezing and relaxing pressure as you move away a star like drop is formed. This procedure is continued around the entire edge of the cake as illustrated. The tiny drop flowers were made up ahead of time on waxed paper in pastel pink royal icing. Starting at the bottom tier, small mounds of icing are piped around the side of the cake to simulate a draped effect. The drop flowers which have been made up beforehand are then placed on the mound of icing. These should start out small and gradually build up and then diminish in width as you come back up to the cake edge.

Pastel green leaves are worked around into the flower garland to cover up any rough edges.

At the base of the next tier, six small mounds of icing are piped on the cake. Pastel green stems and leaves are then worked from the mound. Using the same pastel pink drop flowers, the mound is then covered to simulate a bouquet.

The flowers for the top piece are pink and white mums. These were made from royal icing using a No. 16 tube and a nail covered with a square of waxed paper. This entire top piece may be made up in advance and placed on the cake after decorating. Using this method the bride may slip a spatula knife underneath and slip it off and save it for a keepsake.

A small cardboard circle is used for the base. A mound of icing is piped in the center of the cardboard circle approximately 2½ inches high. The flowers are then placed into position using the colors and sizes to give the top piece a natural life-like effect. Pastel green leaves were then worked around the flowers.

This is a two-tiered cake. Each tier being made up of three layers. The first tier has a diameter of 10 inches and the second has a diameter of 6 inches.

SQUARED BASE WITH DOUBLE RINGED TOP

This is a 12 inch square base, a 10 inch round, and a 6 inch round.

Each tier is made up of three layers.

The border work is illustrated in steps under *Cake Borders*. After the borders are completed, the cake is decorated with tiny pink drop flowers which were made from royal icing using the No. 30 star tube. These are made up on waxed paper and allowed to dry.

The corners of the bottom tier were decorated with small ruffles of pink netting. A small mound of icing is then piped in the corner and draped down over the side of the cake. This is covered with tiny pink drop flowers and green leaves.

The double wedding ring may be made by your florist to carry out any particular flower arrangement that you desire.

"SWEET SUE" CAKE

Featuring a large tilted bell. A simple shell border, double dropped string border, lattice scallop border, fluted garland border, colonial scroll border and reverse shell border decorate this little beauty. Dainty pink roses between the two tiers and tiny clusters of sweetpeas around the bell give a fantasia-like appearance.

ROSE BOUQUET

A four tiered wedding cake with a double wedding ring top piece. The unique and unusual idea on this cake is the use of roses starting at the base and winding up around the cake. These roses are made up ahead of time and placed on the cake after they dry.

GOOD LUCK WEDDING CAKE

A full garland border with fluted edge and lattice work make up the base of this wedding cake. A large rose vine and buds were worked around on the bottom tier. The sugar bells are dipped in silver dragees. The horseshoe top piece (of gumpaste) completes this lovely design.

DOUBLE WEDDING RING

These two ring cakes were iced with a fine layer of buttercream and then covered by pouring fondant over the entire cake. One small tipped bell covered with silver dragees was placed in the center of each ring. The bride and groom are placed in the middle with a bouquet of roses and lilies of the valley working around the sides of the cakes. Two dainty love birds were piped in front of each ring completing the double wedding ring cake.

DOUBLE HEART CAKE

Two heart cakes were placed side by side and trimmed with a simple shell border using the No. 30 star tube. Two dainty slippers of sugar are filled with tiny rosebuds and placed on top of the two heart cakes. The cake top was then finished off with a spray of small pink roses with lilies of the valley in the background.

CHAPTER XIV

Spun and Pulled Sugar

SPUN SUGAR

One piece of equipment you must have in order to make spun sugar properly is a "shaker." This shaker is a four inch square of wood, one inch thick. Fifty 3-inch nails are driven through the wood ½ inch apart.

SPUN SUGAR RECIPE
2 lbs. granulated sugar
1 lb. corn syrup
1 pint water

METHOD

Mix together well. Cook to 290°. While cooking, the sides of the pan should be washed down at least 2 times using hot water and a brush. This eliminates the crystals that form on the side of the pan. Remove from heat and add coloring.

To spin the sugar, two long sticks are placed on a table about 1½ feet apart, extending over the table as illustrated. Stand on a chair to be at a proper height to spin the sugar. Hold pan in the left hand. Dip the shaker down into the candy, lift it up, and let it drain off slightly. Lift the sugar above the sticks and shake back and forth vigorously with a series of long movements. The sugar will fall in fine strands over the sticks. Continue until you have the amount shown in the illustration.

The sugar is then lifted off and placed on a table. Continue until all the cooked sugar is used up. After completing the spun sugar, it may be put in a large air-tight can covered with paper and tightly sealed with a lid. In cool dry weather it will last indefinitely. One use of spun sugar is the Spun Sugar Nest. These are made by taking a small amount of spun sugar — working directly on a table with both hands. The spun sugar is shaped to simulate a nest. These may be used as ice cream dishes. A dipper of ice cream is placed in the center, with a little whipped cream and a cherry to top it off. DO NOT pour sauce on as it will melt your spun sugar. Make up this dessert *just* before serving because melting ice cream will also damage your spun sugar. A large nest is made in the same manner and may be tied with a pulled sugar· ribbon and bow. This nest may be used as a centerpiece, to hold mint patties, or chocolates, etc. Another use of spun sugar is to place it around the base of wedding cakes.

PULLED SUGAR EQUIPMENT

A small brass screen with a 40 to 60 gauge mesh is used to lay the candy on while working pulled sugar. The *electric heater* is a standard home heater with the protective guard removed from the front. The heater is used to keep the batch of candy soft and pliable. The small *leaf mold* shown on the next page is made of lead. Once a leaf is pulled out it is pressed into the mold producing the veins and indentations of a leaf. We use a *scissors* to cut the pulled sugar ribbons, bows, etc.

A *canvas strip* approximately 3 feet long and 14 inches wide is used to stretch out ribbons and bows. A *marble slab* is used for pouring batches of candy on. Although marble is the ideal surface for pulled sugar work, you may use porcelain, a large cookie sheet or Formica. A surface about one foot wide and two feet long is needed for the amount of candy given in the following recipe.

PULLED SUGAR RECIPE

¾ cup water
3 cups granulated sugar
¼ teaspoon cream of tartar

Bring water to a boil, add dry ingredients and mix well. Cook quickly to 312° washing batch down with a brush and warm water three times while cooking to eliminate crystals on side of pan. Do not stir while cooking.

Remove from heat and pour on greased marble slab. If you use porcelain, Formica or large cookie sheet instead of marble, be sure to follow the steps outlined here:

When the batch reaches 312° remove from heat and place pan in cold water for two minutes. Stir constantly to keep the candy from hardening on the sides of the pan. Pour candy on surface heavily greased with lard. As the edges of the batch cool, lift them toward the center of the mass using a metal scraper or spatula knife. Continue turning the edges of the batch inward and work the candy to another area of the surface in order to prevent sticking and to hasten cooling.

170

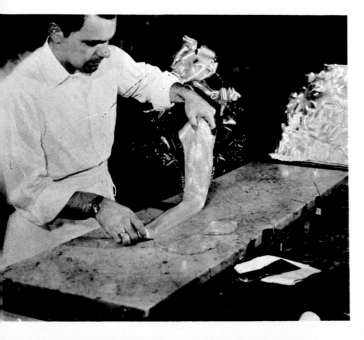

PULLING CANDY

When the sugar is cool enough to handle, roll it into a ball and pull. Each piece should be pulled about 20 times. The sugar will soon take on a sheen and become whiter and whiter. If colored candy is desired, a small portion of paste color may be folded in before the batch is pulled. Do not grease your hands before pulling sugar.

WORKING THE BATCH ON THE SCREEN

The batch is divided into two portions and is placed on the screen directly before the electric heater. The candy must be kept at a workable consistency. While working with one portion, keep the other portion of candy warm and pliable in front of the heater. If the candy you are working with becomes too stiff, switch to the warm piece.

As we progress from a leaf to a little wild flower, yellow jonquil, sweet pea, calla lily, orchid and a rose, you will notice that all the petals are pulled from the candy in the same manner. They all start by looking like a leaf. Then by using your thumb and fingers and shaping the leaf and pulling slightly all the different petals are made. It is very important that you learn to make a leaf properly. Once leaf-making is mastered the rest of the flowers can be made without too much difficulty.

Make sure you keep the candy soft enough to work with. This is why we divide our batches into 3 parts. While you are working with one piece and it tends to get hard, the other two pieces are warmed directly in front of the heater. While working with the candy, continue moving the pieces around to maintain as even a temperature as possible through the candy.

LEAVES

To make a leaf the candy is first stretched out or thinned down. This is done by stretching with both hands. The left thumb is placed in the stretched candy and pulled out. After pulling the leaf out with the thumb as illustrated, cut the leaf at an angle with a pair of scissors. The leaf is then pressed on a mold giving a veined and realistic look.

LEAVES

Illustrated are four types of leaves: the first is a plain leaf; the second is three leaves placed together on a stem; the third is a large oak leaf. To obtain the un- even effect on the sides, the leaf is pulled out slightly with the fingers. The same is true of the last and smaller leaf.

WILD FLOWER

Any bright colors may be used. The center is a small ball of sugar. In making the individual petal as in Step 1, the candy is stretched thin. The left thumb is inserted in the candy and pulled out. Notice the petal resembles a small leaf. The petal is either cut off or snapped off. We use the method of snapping to save time. To do this pull the petal out and squeeze the end together between the thumb and forefinger. Turn the hand and pull away from the batch thus snapping the petal off to a point. When the six small petals are made they are stuck to the center by taking each petal and touching it to the heater coil and then touching it to the center. The six petals are put on as illustrated, finishing your first simple flower.

SWEET PEA

The sweet pea is made up of 3 petals. Each petal simulates a small leaf and is slightly curved to the shape of the thumb. The petals are pulled out and placed back-to-back. Then a green leaf is put on the base of the 3 petals completing the sweet pea.

YELLOW JONQUIL

The center is made by pulling out a strip of candy 2 inches long and 1 inch wide. One side of this strip is ruffled up using the thumb and forefinger. After the ruffle is made the strip is formed into a cone. The six petals that make up the yellow jonquil are pulled out much like the wild flower and are made longer. Each petal should have a slight point. This is made after the petal is pulled out. Using the thumb and forefinger pinch the tip of the petal and pull slightly to a point. Upon completing the six petals, they are stuck on as described under *Wild Flowers*.

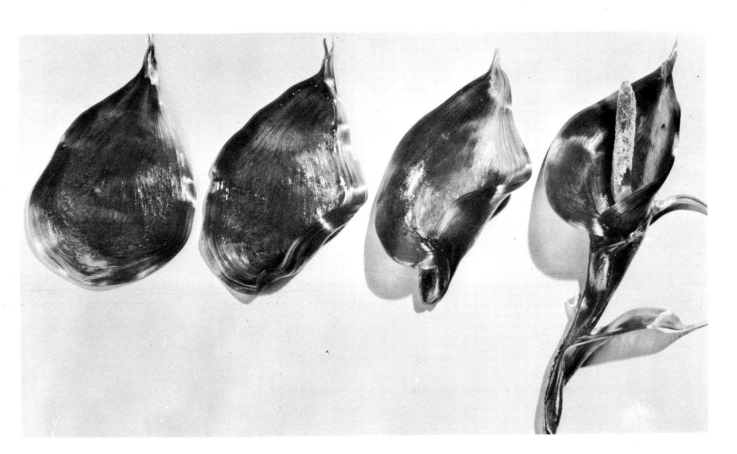

CALLA LILY

The Calla lily is made of white pulled sugar. The first step is to make a large leaf about 3 inches long and 2½ inches wide as illustrated in Step 1. To form the calla lily, the right forefinger is placed down in the corner of the large leaf. Step 2: The right side of the leaf is wrapped around the finger and slightly turned back. A long green stem and two narrow leaves are then put on. The stamen is made by pulling out a narrow piece of candy, moistening it and rolling it in yellow sugar. Touch the end of the stamen to the heater coil and place in the calla lily.

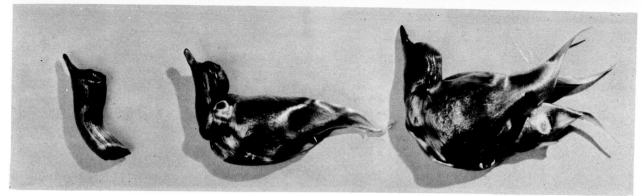

PULLED SUGAR BIRD

A length of candy 1½ inches long, ½ inch in diameter is cut off at an angle while still warm. The cut-off part is squeezed down to form the bill as illustrated. A long narrow leaf is then pulled out and while still soft is stuck to the lower portion of the head that forms the neck. Another long, wing shaped leaf is pulled out and placed on the opposite side. Thus the body is formed. Two more of these long leaf shaped wings are pulled out and put on in the same manner at a slight angle. This completes the bird.

THE EASTER LILY

This flower is made of white pulled sugar. Each petal is much like a leaf. After the petal is pulled out, the round portion of the petal is pinched and pulled slightly to give it a pointed edge. The second petal is pulled out and immediately stuck to the first petal at a slight angle. This procedure is followed until 6 petals are assembled as illustrated. If you work quickly the candy should remain soft. The petals are then put together forming a cup. Should the petals become hard, put them in front of the heater until they have softened. Then fold them over and form the cup. Hold this cup at the base and pull the ends of each petal slightly forming the Easter Lily. Three yellow stamens of pulled sugar are then placed in the flower. This flower is a little difficult to make because it must be formed after the petals are completed.

174

THE POINSETTIA

The poinsettia is made in bright red with a deep yellow center. A small dab of candy is first pulled out of the batch. The petals of the poinsettia are long narrow leaves. After each petal is pulled out it is squeezed slightly and curved. Six petals are used around the base and three around the upper portion. These were stuck on after hardening. Three tiny yellow bell shapes were pulled out of the bright yellow sugar and placed in the center completing the poinsettia.

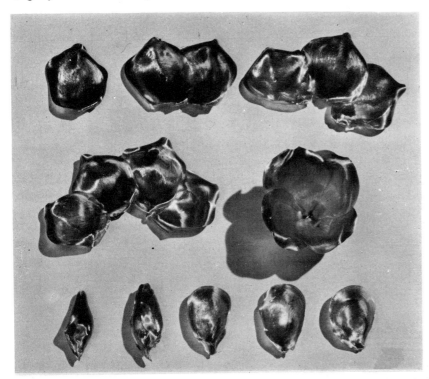

THE AMERICAN BEAUTY ROSE

The American Beauty is made with a deep red tint. After stretching the candy to thin it down, put your left thumb in and pull down and out. This tends to wrap or curve the sugar around your thumb. Cut petal off or snap it off. Then at the top, with both thumbs and both forefingers, roll the two sides of the petal back slightly. This forms a true rose petal. Four more petals are made in this manner and stuck together as each petal is formed. They should form a half circle. The petals are then put together as shown in the next step forming the center of the rose.

The bud is formed by pulling out a petal and wrapping it around the thumb and then rolling it slightly. Another small petal is pulled out and wrapped around the first petal. Three more petals are pulled out much like the rose petal except the tips are not rolled back. Six more individual petals are then pulled out. These are worked around the outside of the rose to put the rose together. The finished rosebud is touched to the heater coil and stuck down into the center of the four petals already put together. The three narrow petals are then heated in the same manner and placed around the bud forming the inside of the rose. The six individual petals that are not illustrated are fastened to the bottom of this by touching them to the heater coil briefly and placing the petal directly under the center. Your American Beauty Rose is now formed. A long green stem and bud are used to give a life-like effect.

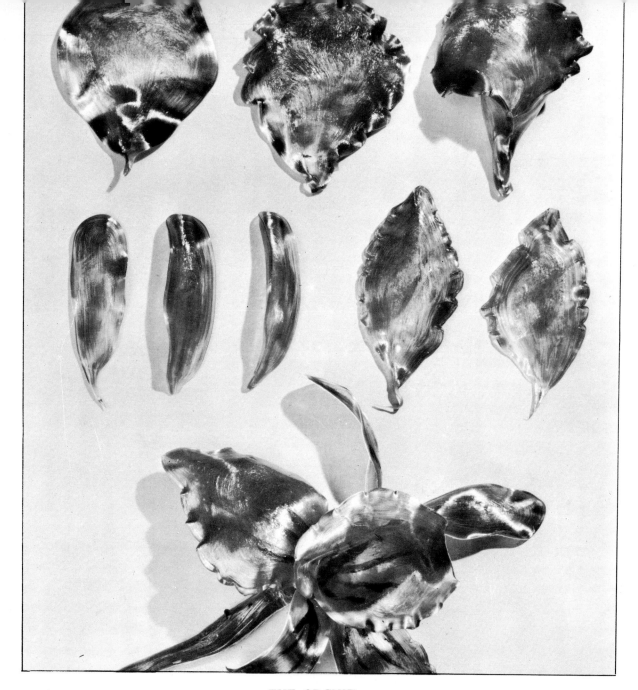

THE ORCHID

The top row illustrates the center portion of the orchid. First, a large leaf-like petal is pulled out much like the calla lily. The outside of this leaf is ruffled slightly. This large ruffled leaf is rolled into a cup shape by placing the right index finger at the point of the leaf and by rolling the candy around it forming the center. The three narrow leaves or petals of the orchid are pulled out in the same manner as the poinsettia. The two larger orchid petals next to them are pulled out and the edges ruffled slightly with the thumb and index finger. The six sections of the orchid are fastened together by heating each individual petal and sticking it to a base, completing the orchid as illustrated. All of these petals should be curved slightly. This is done while the petal is still somewhat soft. This orchid is made in purple and white with a long green stem.

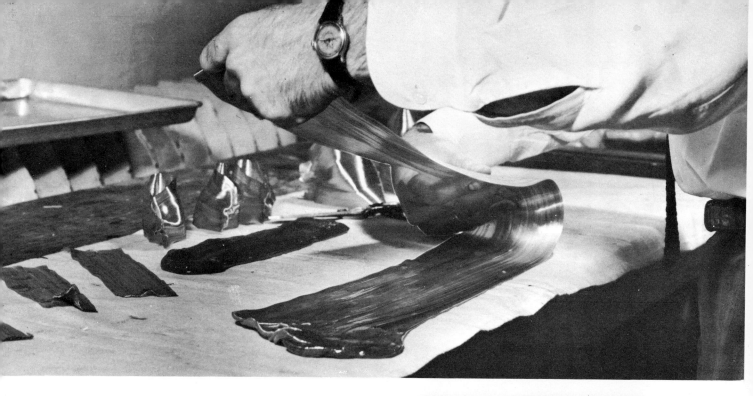

PULLING SUGAR RIBBONS AND BOWS

After working with pulled sugar, you can understand flower making is time consuming. Therefore, when decorating a cake completely in pulled sugar it is to your advantage to cover most of the cake with ribbons and bows. This can be done quickly and still give the cake a decorative appearance.

There are two types of ribbon that we use on the cake: The solid color ribbon, and the striped ribbon. In decorating a cake, the ribbons and bows are made first because the ribbon candy must be soft and pliable to be handled properly. To keep the candy from sticking, the ribbons are pulled or stretched on a heavy piece of canvas. Pulling ribbons takes practice. You'll encounter most of your difficulties with the candy hardening before you finish pulling the ribbon. Learn to work quickly. The finer the ribbon, the higher the gloss obtained.

A piece of candy about 7 inches long and 2 inches wide is cut from the batch. It is placed on the canvas and stretched out to about twice its length. The ribbon candy is folded over side by side, doubling the width. Then stretch and fold over again. This procedure is repeated 3 or 4 times, working very quickly, until a thin shiny length of ribbon is obtained. The ribbon should be 3 feet long. Cut into 6 inch pieces and fold over making up the bows.

Picture above illustrates the bows being pulled. In the foreground are the cut pieces and also the folded ribbons. This same procedure of pulling the ribbon out is used for making the bands that encircle the cake tiers. These bands are made to the desired width and cut off with a scissors. The ribbon is lifted while still soft and put around the cake.

CONSTRUCTING A BOW

After the large band of ribbon is placed on a cake a thin circle of ribbon candy 3 inches in diameter is fastened on. Each section of bow that has already been made up is touched to the heater coil and attractively placed on the circular base. Five or six are used for the outside and four for the inside. This completes the bow.

177

RIBBON STRIPING

To demonstrate this ribbon striping we used red and white ribbon candy. A strip of red candy six inches by two and a half inches was taken from the batch. Then a strip of white candy six inches by one inch was placed next to it. Because the two are warm, they will stick together. The candy is then pulled out to twice the normal size and cut in half. The white sides are placed together as shown. The white strip is then in the middle. This piece of candy is again pulled to twice its length and cut in half. This time the red sides are placed together. Now you have two red stripes. The candy is again pulled out and cut in half. Again the halves are placed side by side giving four narrow stripes. Stretch the candy again, cut in five inch lengths and fold as illustrated.

EASTER LILY SPRAY

The Easter Lily Spray is made like the other cake top layouts. A long narrow leaf is used with the Easter Lily. The flowers are placed side by side giving this cake top a natural look.

JONQUIL SPRAY

This 12 inch cake top was first bordered in tube work. Four green stems were pulled out of the pulled sugar and placed on the cake as illustrated. After the yellow jonquils were made up, they were heated on the under side and placed in position on the stems. Two love birds were then added.

SWEET PEA CLUSTER

For this cake top four clusters of sweet peas were used. Before the clusters are put on, leaves are worked in. The sweet peas are slightly heated and then put on the leaves in clusters.

POINSETTIA CAKE

The poinsettia spray is made by pulling out three long green stems and cutting them off. The underside of the poinsetta is heated and fastened to the stem. Five long, narrow green leaves are then pulled out and placed on the stems.

ROSE CAKE

One long stemmed American Beauty Rose with buds and leaves complete this cake top. The border of this cake top is made by pulling two long pieces of candy out and rolling them together on a canvas.

179

ROSE SPRAY

For this floral layout four long stems were pulled out and cut to the desired length. While still soft the stems were placed in position. One large rose at the base and four small roses make up this floral piece. The roses, buds, and leaves were made up in advance and stuck to the cake top. An inscription may be written in the same manner as on a tube decorated cake.

CANDY CANES

To prepare these delightful decorations, pull a piece of candy 3 ft. long and about ¼ inch in diameter from each of two batches of contrasting colors. The two candy strips are then placed side by side on the canvas. Hold one end fast and roll the other end in an arc to create a rope effect with the two colored strips. This length of candy is then cut into desired lengths for the candy canes. The rope of colored candy may also be used as a cake border as shown here.

180

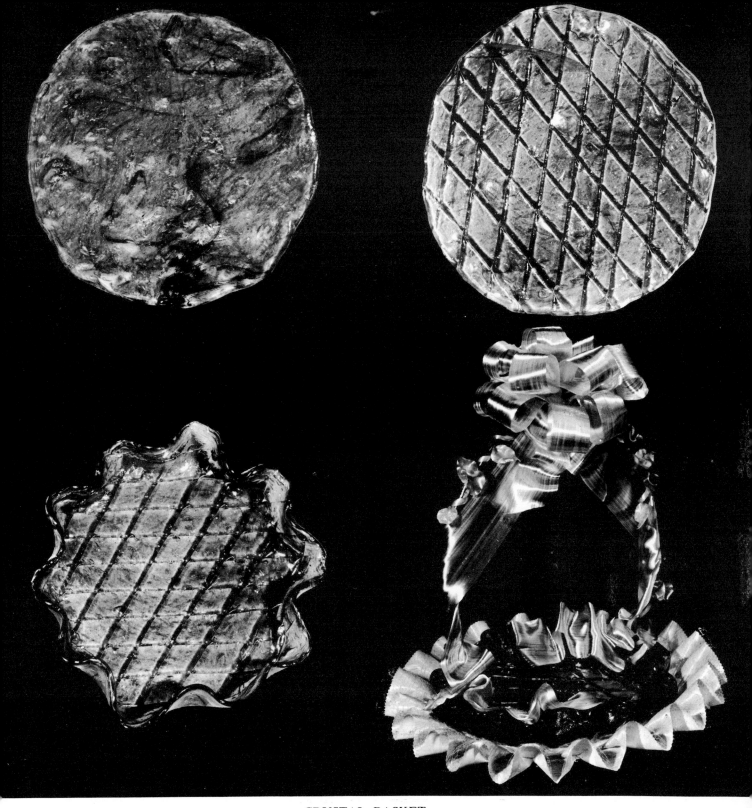

CRYSTAL BASKET

For the Crystal Basket we use the same recipe as for Pulled Sugar Work. Coloring is put in before the batch is poured on the marble slab. The crystal look is obtained by leaving the sugar in its natural state (by not pulling sugar). A piece of sugar candy weighing about 1 lb. is rolled with a rolling pin to form a circle of 8 inches in diameter. While the candy is still soft, the criss-cross indentations are added by pressing with the blade of a knife. The edges are then fluted up as you would the edges of a pie. For the handle of the basket, a heavy clothes hanger was straightened out and clipped off at a 2 foot length. Then we bend the wire to the desired curve and run it through soft sugar candy. Two pieces of soft candy were stuck at the base of the wire and then touched to the electric heater. The wire is then placed in position on the basket. The ribbon is then pulled out in delicate pink and wrapped around the handle. The bow is made up ahead of time on a piece of sugar candy. After hardening, it is fastened to the top of the basket as illustrated.

181

OPEN SWAN

To be used as a centerpiece for weddings or showers. The swan is made up of four sections. The neck is pulled out of a piece of candy to about 12 inches long and then cut off at a 45° angle. Using your fingers and thumb, the head is formed from this 45° cutoff. The long piece of candy is shaped in a question mark as illustrated. The two wings are 9 inches long and 4 inches wide at the longest points. These are rolled out of sugar and cut to form this leaf. Before hardening they are shaped into a curved effect. The base is slightly smaller than the wings and is turned up at the end. After the four sections are hardened the neck is stuck to the base. The two wings are stuck to the neck. Feathers are placed on beginning at the back of the wing and working forward. They resemble long fine leaves. A dainty pink bow with streamers was tied around the neck of the swan. Pastel pink roses were worked around the base. This swan has an open back.

CHAPTER XV

Candy Making

We have compiled a delightful selection of recipes for you including recipes of all nations, many that you may never have heard of and many old favorites too.

These fine recipes are *no accident*, they are carefully tested and reliable—leaving out any guesswork on your part—no more sugary fudges or candies that won't crisp properly. There will never again be a "hope it turns out O. K. this time" attitude.

Just remember these two important points—(1) Measure accurately (2) Use a candy thermometer, a temperature variation of two or three degrees may ruin the texture of your batch.

Use your candy thermometer and you will know exactly when your candy is ready.

Then what fun you will have surprising your friends with some of the fanciest candies, dipped or stuffed fruit or even that old stand-by creamy fudge.

This chapter will offer you fun and good eating.

CREAM FONDANT

This recipe is the foundation of many fine pieces of candy.

3 cups granulated sugar
1½ cups water
1 tablespoon corn syrup
pinch cream of tartar

Combine sugar, water, corn syrup and cream of tartar. Bring to a boil and wash down crystals around sides of the pan with a small brush. Cook to 238 degrees and immediately pour on platter or porcelain table top. When luke warm, scrape fondant with a wooden scraper toward the center of the platter. Work with scraper until creamed and stiff. Knead until free from lumps. Place in a covered container until ripened, about 24 hours. This may be kept for 2 weeks.

The fondant may be re-heated in a double boiler.

When good and warm, use table fork for dipping almonds, dates and California grapes.

Strawberries may be held by the stem and dipped half way in the fondant and then placed on waxed paper.

Add a cup of chopped walnuts to fondant, blend in 1 teaspoon vanilla, and drop from a spoon for fondant cream kisses.

For maple kisses, use a few drops of mapelene flavor and burnt sugar.

To make a mint pattie basket, two mints are stuck together with a dot of royal icing. Place the two mints that have been stuck together into warm fondant of a contrasting color. These should be dipped about ⅓ of the way into the fondant. Lift out and place upright to drain on waxed paper. The softer fondant will run down forming a wide base in the contrasting color, thus holding the mints in the upright position, giving them a basket effect. Using a small cone and a No. 3 tube, the handle is then piped over the top of the mint. Small flowers and leaves may be piped out of the sides of the basket as illustrated.

If you desire, you may place a small place card between the mints before dipping. Using this arrangement, the mint pattie baskets are used for place card holders.

PEPPERMINT PATTIES

1 lb. Fondant

STEP I

Place the fondant in a double boiler and stir intermittently while heating. The correct temperature of the fondant for making patties is about 160 degrees.

The coloring and flavoring is added to the fondant while heating in the double boiler. Any flavoring may be added to the desired taste.

STEP II

After heating to the correct temperature, the fondant is poured into the funnel with the stick placed at the bottom of the funnel.

The patties are dropped on the rubber mat or the wax paper as follows: By lifting the stick up, the fondant drops out forming the patty. A series of patties are made by an up and down motion of the stick while moving the funnel.

Dropping out mints using candy funnel.

SPECIAL COMMENTS

1. Care must be exercised to get the proper temperature of the fondant. If the fondant is too hot, the mints will not hold their oval shape when dropped from the funnel. They will be very flat and distorted instead of round.

2. Another sign of overheating is that white spots will form on the patty.

3. A rubber mat is recommended in order to form corrugations on the bottom of patties. Corrugations help prevent the patties from sticking together when stacked. Patties may be dropped on waxed paper as illustrated.

POWDERED SUGAR MINTS

2½ cups granulated sugar
1 cup water
pinch cream of tartar
2 cups powdered sugar
mint oil

Combine sugar, water and cream of tartar and bring to a boil at 230 degrees. Always wash down crystals from sides of pan with small brush dipped in water. Add 2 cups powdered sugar and a few drops of mint oil and beat vigorously with a small hand whip until creamy, about 2 or 3 minutes.

Drop round patties on waxed paper from the end of a spoon. Or pour mixture into a funnel and allow drops to fall as illustrated. A stick of about ½ inch in diameter is used in the funnel. By moving the stick up and down you control the flow through the funnel and the size of the mints.

FRUIT DELIGHT

½ cup granulated sugar
½ cup brown sugar
1 cup corn syrup
½ cup water
3 cups finely chopped cocoanut
½ cup walnut pieces
½ cup candied cherries
½ cup raisins
½ teaspoon salt
1 teaspoon vanilla
1 teaspoon butter

Combine sugar, corn syrup and water. Cook without stirring to 240 degrees. Thicken with raisins, cocoanut, nuts and cherries. Add vanilla, salt and butter. Butter and sprinkle cookie sheet with fine cocoanut. Spread fruit delight ¾ inch thick on cookie sheet sprinkled with cocoanut. Sprinkle cocoanut on top. When cool slice into 1 inch squares.

ITALIAN TRONIAE

2 cups honey
1 cup granulated sugar
½ cup corn syrup
½ cup of water
½ cup pistachio nuts
½ cup candied cherries
3 egg whites
½ teaspoon salt
1 teaspoon butter

Combine honey, granulated sugar, corn syrup and water. Cook and stir to 272 degrees. Add syrup slowly to 3 well beaten egg whites. Beat until good and stiff. Fold in with nuts, cherries, butter and salt. Spread 1 inch thick on buttered cookie sheet, dusted with flour. Cut in oblongs, 1 inch long and ½ inch wide using large table knife. Wrap pieces of candy in waxed paper.

CREAM O'MINTS KISSES

4 cups sugar
¼ teaspoon cream of tartar
1½ cups water
4 to 5 drops peppermint oil
1 teaspoon butter

Combine sugar, cream of tartar and water and boil to 270 degrees without stirring. Wash sides down with brush dipped in water at least three times while boiling. Add butter without stirring, boil ½ minute longer. Pour on well greased pan dusted with flour. When cool, turn up edges. Pour in peppermint oil and pull when cool enough to handle. Pull about 75 times. Dust table top with powdered sugar, roll and pull out to size of index finger. Cut in small pieces ¾ inch long. These may be wrapped in waxed paper or allowed to dry. These kisses are at their best after 24 hours.

MEXICAN PANOCHA

3 cups light brown sugar
1 cup granulated sugar
¼ lb. butter
2 tablespoons corn syrup
1 cup coffee cream
½ teaspoon salt
1 teaspoon mapelene flavor
1 cup pecan pieces

Combine sugar, butter, corn syrup, salt and cream and stir constantly. Cook to 236 degrees. Remove from heat and stir vigorously with a wooden spoon. When mixture begins to get heavy and creamy, add pecan pieces and spread on buttered cookie sheet about ¼ inch thick. Mark and cut in 1½ inch squares.

ENGLISH TOFFEY

1 lb. butter
3 cups granulated sugar
1 cup roasted chopped almonds
1 lb. dark sweet chocolate

Melt butter and add sugar stirring constantly until golden brown or 290 degrees. Spread on greased cookie sheet and cool.

Shave and melt 1 lb. dark sweet chocolate in double boiler and allow to cool. Before setting, spread half on top of toffey and sprinkle roasted almonds on chocolate. Place in refrigerator to set. After setting turn over and pour remaining chocolate over top and again sprinkle with almonds.

The toffey now has chocolate almond coating on top and bottom.

CHOCOLATE ALMOND BARK

Shave and melt 1 lb. dark sweet chocolate in double boiler. Let chocolate stand and cool. Before it sets, add 1 cup of chopped roasted almonds. Spread on cookie sheet lined with waxed paper. Use table fork stroking back and forth to create a tree bark design. Place in refrigerator for 2 hours.

FRENCH BON BON CENTERS

1 cup honey

1 cup corn syrup

Boil to 230 degrees. Stiffen with 4 or 5 cups chopped fine cocoanut. When cool roll into small balls for dipping. These centers are for French bon bons and may be dipped in fondant or chocolate.

COCOANUT MARSHMALLOW

Chop 5 cups cocoanut very fine and brown in oven. Take 1 cup corn syrup and 1 teaspoon butter and heat. Using a small dishpan, place 8 or 10 marshmallows in bottom and pour a little hot syrup on them and roll marshmallows in syrup then in toasted cocoanut.

MARSHMALLOW

3 cups granulated sugar

2 cups corn syrup

1 cup water

1¼ cup water

1 oz. powdered gelatine (1 pkg.)

1 teaspoon vanilla

½ teaspoon salt

Combine sugar, corn syrup and water. Cook to 240 degrees.

Dissolve gelatine in 1¼ cup cold water and bring to a boil. Add sugar, syrup, vanilla and salt and beat for 10 minutes. Line cookie sheet with white or brown paper (do not use waxed paper). Spread 1 inch thick. Must set for 5 hours after spreading. Sprinkle powdered sugar on top to prevent sticking.

After the marshmallow has set for the 5 hour period, turn over and moisten the brown paper on which it was poured. This will make the paper peel off the marshmallow.

After peeling off the paper, sprinkle the top again with powdered sugar and cut in strips about an inch thick. Turn each strip over and cut in 1 inch squares.

PECAN GLACE

2 cups granulated sugar
1½ cups corn syrup
1 cup water
2 cups pecan pieces
1 teaspoon butter
½ teaspoon salt

Combine sugar, corn syrup and water. Cook without stirring to 300 degrees. Reduce heat and add pecans, butter and salt. Mix well, pour on to greased cookie sheet.

RED TAFFY APPLES

4 cups granulated sugar
½ cup corn syrup
1½ cups water
1 teaspoon wild cherry flavor
red color
8 medium sized apples (with meat skewers)

Combine sugar, corn syrup and water. Boil to 285 degrees. Add wild cherry flavor and coloring. Dip apples into hot syrup and twirl throwing the excess candy off the apple. Stand on a buttered cookie sheet.

CARAMEL APPLES, or Pan Caramels

3 cups granulated sugar
2 cups corn syrup
1 cup coffee cream
1 cup evaporated milk
1 tablespoon butter
1 level teaspoon salt
1 teaspoon vanilla

Combine sugar, corn syrup, coffee cream and butter. Stir constantly and heat. When mixture begins to boil, add cup of evaporated milk. Cook to 242 degrees. Remove from heat, add salt and vanilla. Dip apples into caramel twirling apples to throw off the excess caramel and stand on greased cookie sheet. For pan caramels, pour into greased cookie sheet dusted with flour.

PUFFED RICE PEANUT CANDY

1 cup water
1 cup granulated sugar
1 cup brown sugar
1½ cups corn syrup
1 cup Spanish roasted peanuts
2 cups puffed rice
1 teaspoon butter
1 teaspoon salt
1 teaspoon baking soda

Combine water, sugar, corn syrup and boil to 290 degrees. Reduce heat, add butter, peanuts and puffed rice. Mix well and boil for 2 minutes longer. Remove from heat, add baking soda and salt. Stir well. Pour on to a buttered greased cookie sheet and spread in a layer about an inch thick.

PEANUT BRITTLE

2 cups granulated sugar
1½ cups corn syrup
1 cup water
2 cups salted peanuts
1 teaspoon baking soda
½ teaspoon salt
1 teaspoon butter

Combine sugar, corn syrup, water. Boil without stirring to 300 degrees. Add butter and peanuts, reduce heat and stir for 1 minute over low heat. Remove from heat and add salt and baking soda. Mix well. Spread in thin layer on buttered cookie sheet.

WILD CHERRY LOLLIPOPS

2 cups granulated sugar
1 cup corn syrup
1 cup water
1 tablespoon wild cherry flavoring
½ teaspoon salt
red coloring to suit

Combine sugar, corn syrup and water. Cook without stirring to 300 degrees. Add flavoring, salt and coloring. Drop with tablespoon on wooden meat skewer sticks about three inches apart and the size of a dollar, on greased cookie sheet dusted with flour.

VANILLA SALT WATER TAFFY KISSES

3 cups granulated sugar
2 cups corn syrup
1 cup water
1 tablespoon butter
½ teaspoon salt
1 teaspoon vanilla

Combine sugar, corn syrup, butter and water. Boil and stir to 260 degrees. Add salt and vanilla. Pour on pan (greased and dusted with flour) to cool. Pull with greased hands about 75 times. The more you pull the lighter the taffy. Roll out on flour dusted table about the thickness of index finger. Cut in small pieces about an inch long and wrap in waxed paper.

CARAMEL CORN

2 cups light brown sugar
1 cup granulated sugar
4 tablespoons corn syrup
1 teaspoon salt
1 cup water
1½ gal. popped corn

Combine sugar, corn syrup and water. Boil without stirring to 285 degrees. It will be necessary to wash down sides of pan with brush dipped in water. When syrup has reached 285 degrees, add butter and salt. Pour on warm popped corn, using table forks for mixing. Spread on pan.

BUTTERSCOTCH SQUARES

4 cups granulated sugar
1 cup corn syrup
1 cup water
1 tablespoon butter
pinch salt

Combine sugar, corn syrup and water. Cook to 300 degrees. Add butter, salt and mix thoroughly. Pour on heavily greased cookie sheet. Mark in squares.

CALIFORNIA CHOCOLATE CREAM FUDGE

3 cups granulated sugar
3 tablespoons corn syrup
1 cup coffee cream
1 tablespoon butter
2 sq. chocolate (shaved)
1 cup pecans
pinch salt
1 teaspoon vanilla

Combine sugar, corn syrup, coffee cream, butter and chocolate. Stir constantly and heat to 238 degrees. Remove from heat and stir vigorously until heavy and creamy, and add pecans, vanilla and salt. Pour into a buttered greased pan about half inch deep.

OLD FASHIONED DIVINITY KISSES

½ cup water
2 cups granulated sugar
2 tablespoons corn syrup (white)
pinch cream of tartar
1 cup chopped walnuts
1 cup chopped dates
2 egg whites
1 teaspoon vanilla
pinch salt

Combine sugar, corn syrup, water and cream of tartar. Cook without stirring and wash down crystals from sides of the pan with small brush dipped in water. Cook to 248 degrees (soft ball test). Have egg whites beaten to a peak. Slowly add syrup and egg whites and beat with mixer for at least 20 minutes until good and heavy. Add 1 teaspoon vanilla and a pinch of salt and then fold in nuts and dates. Allow to set for 1 hour and spoon out on waxed paper.

OLD FASHIONED HOREHOUND STICK

3 cups granulated sugar
½ cup corn syrup
1 cup water
1 tablespoon horehound tea

Combine water and horehound tea and bring to a boil. Let stand 1 hour and strain. Combine sugar and corn syrup with tea. Cook to 290 degrees. Pour on greased cookie sheet or table top. Roll edges in. When cooled sufficiently to handle, pull out in the shape and size of the index finger. Pull out sticks about a yard long, roll round and cut into 4 inch strips with scissors.

NEW ORLEANS PRALINES

2 cups granulated sugar
1 cup brown sugar
1½ cup pecan pieces
1½ cup water
1 teaspoon burnt sugar coloring
1 pinch cream of tartar

Combine all ingredients, bring to boil and wash down sides of pan with brush dipped in water. Boil to 236 degrees, remove from heat and stir for 4 or 5 minutes. Spoon out with large wooden spoon onto waxed paper in patties about 3½ inch in diameter.

Can be wrapped in cellophane paper in individual pieces.

POP CORN BALLS

2 cups granulated sugar
1 cup corn syrup
1 cup water
popped corn
1 tablespoon butter
1 teaspoon salt
1 teaspoon vanilla

Combine water, sugar, corn syrup and cook to 270 degrees. Add butter, mix well, add vanilla and salt. Pour on warmed popped corn. Using 2 table forks, mix by stirring from bottom of bowl up.

Grease hands, and roll into balls of size desired.

You may add coloring when batch has cooked to 270 degrees.

CHEWY FRENCH NUGGET

3 cups granulated sugar
2 cups corn syrup
1½ cups water
1 teaspoon vanilla
1 teaspoon butter
3 egg whites
1 teaspoon almond flavor
1½ cups roasted filberts, chopped
1 level teaspoon salt

Combine sugar, corn syrup, water and boil to 270 degrees. Add slowly to 3 well beaten egg whites. Beat until heavy. Add salt, flavoring, butter and fold in the chopped nuts with a tablespoon. Spread on flour dusted buttered tin ¾ inch thick. Cut in small pieces and wrap in waxed paper. The pieces can be dipped in chocolate if desired.

ANISE SQUARES

2 cups granulated sugar
1 cup corn syrup
1 cup water
1 teaspoon anise oil
5 drops red color

Combine sugar, water, corn syrup and cook without stirring to 300 degrees. Remove from heat and add anise oil and red color. Pour in well greased pans, mark with large knife into 1 inch squares.

MOLASSES PULLED TAFFY

4 cups granulated sugar
1 cup corn syrup
1 cup molasses
1 teaspoon butter
1 level teaspoon salt
1 cup water

Combine sugar, corn syrup, molasses and water. Cook without stirring to 270 degrees. Add butter and salt. Pour on well greased cookie sheet or on table top dusted with flour. When it begins to cool, turn up edges and pull with hands slightly greased. Shape in round rope strips and cut with scissors into 1 inch pieces. Wrap with waxed paper if desired.

ALMOND CRUNCH

3 cups granulated sugar
1½ cups corn syrup
1 cup water
1 tablespoon butter
1 cup chopped roasted almonds
½ level teaspoon salt
1 cup finely chopped cocoanut
1 teaspoon baking soda
1 teaspoon salt

Combine corn syrup and sugar. Boil without stirring to 300 degrees. Add chopped roasted almonds and butter. Reduce heat. When butter is melted, remove from heat and add baking soda and salt. Stir vigorously for ½ minute and pour on a greased cookie sheet sprinkled with chopped cocoanut. Spread thinly and sprinkle cocoanut on top. Roll with a rolling pin. Mark in inch squares with a large knife.

FRENCH PARLUNA FUDGE

1 lb. dark sweet chocolate shaved and melted in double boiler.
When melted, add 1 cup hot coffee cream, pour in slowly. Stir mixture vigorously. Add 1 teaspoon vanilla. Pour on waxed paper ½ inch thick. Sprinkle chopped walnuts or pistachio nuts on top.
Place in refrigerator for 5 hours to set. Cut into 1 inch squares.

BUTTERSCOTCH CORNFLAKES

1 cup brown sugar
1 cup granulated sugar
1½ cup corn syrup
1 cup water
¼ lb. butter
1 teaspoon baking soda
5 cups corn flakes

Combine sugar, corn syrup, water and cook to 300 degrees. Add butter and heat over low flame until all butter is melted. Remove from heat and add baking soda. Then add corn flakes which have been slightly warmed. Spread on cookie sheet ¾ inch thick.

MOLASSES CARAMEL CORN

½ cup brown sugar
1 cup granulated sugar
2 tablespoons corn syrup
1 tablespoon molasses
1 tablespoon butter
½ teaspoon salt
2 cups roasted salted peanuts
popcorn

Combine sugar, corn syrup, water and cook to 285 degrees. Add molasses, butter and salt. Pour over warm popcorn, then add peanuts. Stir all together spreading out on a cookie sheet to cool.

BLACK WALNUT CHEWS

3 cups light brown sugar
1 cup corn syrup
1 teaspoon butter
1 teaspoon salt
1 cup chopped black walnuts
1 cup water

Combine sugar, corn syrup, water and cook to 270 degrees. Remove from heat, add walnuts, butter, salt and mix. Pour on a well greased cookie sheet dusted with flour. Pull with lightly greased hands about 75 times. Shape into a rope and cut with scissors into 1 inch pieces. Wrap in waxed paper.

OPERA CREAMS

4 cups granulated sugar
4 teaspoons corn syrup
1 cup coffee cream
1 teaspoon vanilla
pinch salt
1 cup walnut pieces

Combine sugar, corn syrup, cream and without stirring cook to 238 degrees. Remove from heat and add vanilla, salt and nutmeats and beat vigorously until creamy and heavy. Pour on buttered sheet to cool. Mark in 1 inch squares.

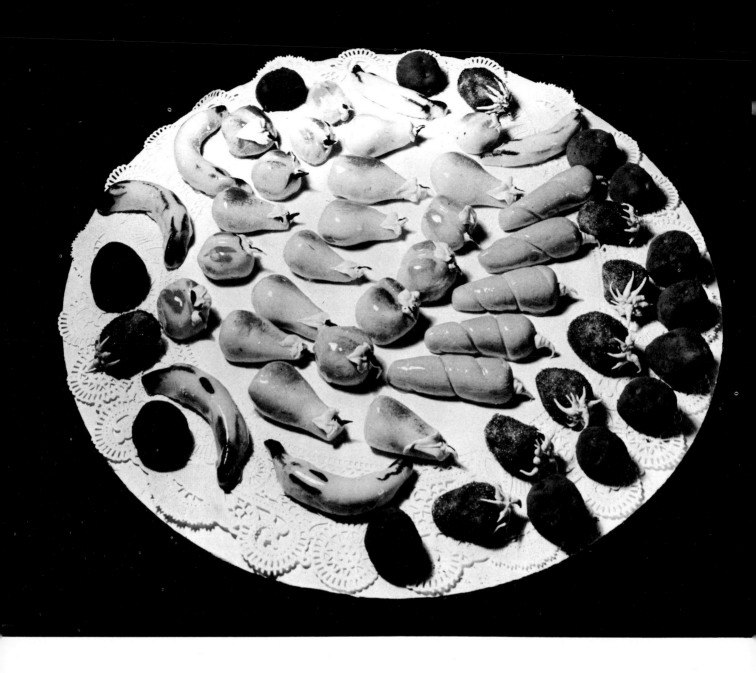

MARZIPAN

The only equipment we use is a stick 5 inches long and ⅛ inch in diameter. This is used for creasing the different pieces of marzipan. Small artificial leaves may be bought for marzipan fruits and vegetables to give them a more realistic appearance. However, because they are not edible, we prefer to make our own.

MARZIPAN RECIPE

1 cup almond paste
2 egg whites (unbeaten)
3 cups powdered sugar
½ teaspoon vanilla or rum flavor

Place almond paste into a bowl and knead by hand. Add egg whites and mix well. Add sugar one cup at a time. Continue kneading and add flavoring. Total mixing time is 15 minutes. Marzipan should feel like a heavy pie dough at its proper consistency. Use powdered sugar when dusting the table to prevent marzipan from sticking. After your Marzipan pieces are finished, brush with a warmed corn syrup to give them a glazed look.

190

When Marzipan is properly made it is about the same consistency as pie dough. Cornstarch is used for dusting to prevent sticking. To obtain a uniform size to your marzipan pieces, roll out a long narrow length of marzipan 2½ feet long and ¾ inch in diameter. Cut into 1¼ inch lengths, as illustrated. If larger pieces of marzipan are desired, cut into 2 inch lengths. For all types of fruits and vegetables the procedure in forming them is almost identical except for slight variations.

PEACHES

Color marzipan a light yellow by working in a touch of yellow paste color. After cutting marzipan into pieces as previously described, roll pieces in your hands to form a ball. Use a narrow length of stick to put on indentation in one side to obtain a peach shape. (Picture No. 2) Leaves, stems and additional color are added later.

PEARS

The same procedure as above is followed, using yellow marzipan. After the ball is formed, it is then worked into a slight cone and narrowed down with the forefinger by rolling.

PUMPKIN

A colorful orange is used for making the pumpkin. The balls are first formed by rolling the small pieces in your hands. Six ridges are made around the upper portion of the ball using your wooden tool. Start the ridges in the middle and work up to the top.

NEW POTATOES

A perfect size to be made in marzipan. It is not necessary to color the marzipan. After rolling the marzipan into various shaped ovals, roll in a moist cloth to dampen slightly. Roll immediately in cocoa powder. The eyes are put in the potatoes by pushing your wooden stick into the finished potato.

STRAWBERRIES

A small amount of red paste color is first worked into the marzipan. After cutting into small pieces and rolling into balls, the strawberry is made like the pear except that it is not as long or narrow as the pear. Granulated sugar is colored red by rubbing sugar and red paste color between the palms of the hands. The strawberries are then moistened with a damp cloth and rolled into the red granulated sugar.

191

BANANA

Color yellow before rolling out your long narrow strip of marzipan. Cut the pieces to lengths of 1½ inches. Roll the pieces to the shape of a banana and then pinch slightly at both ends and serve.

CARROTS

Carrots are made of light orange colored marzipan. Cut your strips into 1½ inch lengths. Roll pieces into balls using the palms of the hands. The carrot is formed by rolling the ball on the table using the first three fingers. One end is larger, the other narrow. Using the back of the knife held at an angle to the carrot, roll the carrot completely. This gives the ridges in the carrot.

APPLES

Color the marzipan a delicate green. Roll into round balls. Using the wood tool, make a slight indentation in the apple to simulate the top. After the molding is complete place the finished pieces on a pan and paint in the following manner. With a soft damp cloth, lightly touch the desired paste color. Rub the cloth over a small portion of the molded fruit. Using this method the color is blended in giving the fruit a natural look.

LEAVES

The artificial stems and leaves are then placed on the molded marzipan. If you care to make your own, use two small cones, one with a 67 leaf tube, the other with a No. 3 tube. The cones are filled with a thinned down green royal icing. As you can see, after making these various marzipan fruits and vegetables, all the different pieces are similar and can be made by anyone after 5 minutes of instruction. Changing color and shapes is all that marzipan work requires.

The color blending should be carried out in the following colors . . .

Yellow peach—touched in red.
Yellow pear—flecked in brown.
Orange pumpkin—no added color.
New potato—rolled in cocoa powder.
Red strawberry—stripe with brush in brown.
Orange carrot—no added color.
Green Apple—touched in red.